LET'S TALK ABOUT POLYGAMY

OTHER BOOKS IN THE
LET'S TALK ABOUT SERIES

Let's Talk about Religion and Mental Health

For more information on the other books
in the Let's Talk About series,
visit DesBook.com/LetsTalk.

LET'S TALK ABOUT POLYGAMY

BRITTANY CHAPMAN NASH

SALT LAKE CITY, UTAH

For Peter and our children, with love.

In memory of my ancestors Prudence Carter, Lucy Williams, Eliza Jerusha Gibbs, Elizabeth Maslen, Oline Amundsdatter, Mary Ann Harding, and Ruth May, who strengthen and inspire me.

Visit us at deseretbook.com

Library of Congress Cataloging-in-Publication Data

Names: Nash, Brittany Chapman, author.
Title: Let's talk about polygamy / Brittany Chapman Nash.
Other titles: Polygamy | Let's talk about (Deseret Book)
Description: Salt Lake City : Deseret Book, 2021. | Series: Let's talk about | Includes bibliographical references. | Summary: "Latter-day Saint historian Brittany Chapman Nash gives a historical overview and explanation of the early practice of polygamy among members of The Church of Jesus Christ of Latter-day Saints"—Provided by publisher.
Identifiers: LCCN 2021012164 | ISBN 9781629728230 (trade paperback)
Subjects: LCSH: Polygamy—Religious aspects—The Church of Jesus Christ of Latter-day Saints—History. | Polygamy—Religious aspects—Mormon Church—History.
Classification: LCC BX8643.P63 N37 2021 | DDC 261.8/3584230882893—dc23
LC record available at https://lccn.loc.gov/2021012164

Printed in the United States of America
PubLitho, Draper, UT

10 9 8 7 6 5 4 3 2 1

CONTENTS

PREFACE

"The past is a foreign country:
they do things differently there."
—L. P. Hartley, 1953

As I sat in the front row of my seventh-grade US history class in the eastern United States, my teacher began discussing the "polygamous Mormons in Utah." My heart pounded. This was my moment to represent my faith as a member of The Church of Jesus Christ of Latter-day Saints. With nerves rushing, I raised my hand and timidly said, "Mormons don't practice polygamy anymore." My teacher acknowledged my assertion, and that brief exchange was my first experience talking about the Latter-day Saint practice of polygamy. I continued to have discussions about polygamy as I grew older, but I dreaded questions on the subject because I knew little about it myself. In my young mind, Latter-day Saints' polygamous past was an embarrassment to reject, a point of misunderstanding to readily correct.

I retained this perception until graduate school when I began to study the life of my great-great-grandmother Ruth May Fox, who was the first wife in a polygamous union. As I rooted through her writings and those of other Latter-day Saint women, I found myself peeking into a world rich with sisterhood and profound faith. These women talked fearlessly about polygamy, a practice they also called plural marriage. My admiration for them stood alongside discomfort as I studied the unfamiliar, difficult, and complex history of plural marriage. Its realities did not fit into the tidy paradigm of Church history that I then understood. I was angry; it seemed unjust that so much sacrifice was asked of such faithful people.

But, as I persisted in learning about polygamy from a breadth of records, I found reconciliation through the experiences and testimonies of those who chose plural marriages. As *they* talked about polygamy, I learned what it meant to trust in God through hard things. The sacrifices they willingly made because of religious conviction moved me, and their commitment to the restored gospel, manifest through their obedience to this principle, ultimately served to strengthen my own faith. My eventual career at the Church History Library, where I specialized in women's history and continued to study plural marriage, only deepened this appreciation.

As we enter the past through a study of Latter-day Saint polygamy, we may feel that we are strangers in a foreign land, gazing into a world very different from our own. Polygamy can be a challenging issue to understand, particularly in the context of our own time and sensibilities, and not every question has an answer. Records clearly indicate that plural marriage was an imperfect system practiced by imperfect individuals. It was vulnerable to abuse, and that cannot be minimized or excused. However, plural marriages made in good faith were the norm, not the exception. Although it may be difficult to understand why Latter-day Saints elected to live polygamously, perhaps we can come to respect their point of view as we learn their stories.

It is my hope to offer a candid and balanced history of polygamy in The Church of Jesus Christ of Latter-day Saints through the voices of those who practiced it and, in the process, offer understanding and reconciliation from a faithful perspective. I hope that the authentic voices of Latter-day Saints will help to ease the fear, shame, and silence that sometimes shrouds this topic and that polygamy will become something we all can talk about.

Brittany Chapman Nash
Salt Lake City, Utah
July 2021

Acknowledgments

I am deeply grateful to Kari Lynne Gillis Roueche, my research assistant; she is an integral part of this book, and it is infinitely richer because of her contribution. My heartfelt thanks to Lisa Olsen Tait, Laurel Thatcher Ulrich, Lynne Larson, Ardis Smith, and Alison Elbrader for their significant roles in shaping this work. My sincere thanks to additional friends' influential expertise: Suzanne Brady, Andrew H. Hedges, Jed Woodworth, Rachel Killebrew, and Ruth Todd. Many thanks to Lisa Roper and to my skillful editor, Alison Palmer, both of Deseret Book. I am thoroughly indebted to Connie Christopher; Madalyn and Calvin Nash; Dane, Barbara, and Cooper Chapman; and Grace Musser for countless hours of childcare and beta-reading. Finally, thank you to Peter Nash, my persevering, supportive husband—strong, solid, unchanging.

INTRODUCTION

PIECING TOGETHER POLYGAMY

The practice of polygamy in The Church of Jesus Christ of Latter-day Saints was a battleground where faith, culture, and commandment collided: to its opponents it was "a rock that need[ed] blowing up with the dynamite of law"; to its adherents it was "the word and will of God."[1] For most people in the Western world, polygamy infringed on the sanctity of monogamous marriage, the foundation upon which society was built.

In other areas of the world, however, polygamy was a normal part of life. Roughly 85 percent of documented societies practiced polygamy in some form, far outnumbering strictly monogamous societies.[2] As Latter-day Saints developed plural marriage, several other groups in nineteenth-century America were experimenting with nontraditional marital and sexual practices, including the Shakers, the Oneida Community, and members of the free-love movement.[3] Still, it was Latter-day Saint polygamy—also called plural marriage, patriarchal marriage, celestial marriage, plurality, or "the Principle"—that prompted the greatest public outrage.*

* Latter-day Saints practiced a form of polygamy called *polygyny*, where a man was married to more than one woman. Because the general term *polygamy* was most often applied to the practice historically, I use the term *polygamy*, instead of the more accurate *polygyny*.

Joseph Smith, the founder and first President of The Church of Jesus Christ of Latter-day Saints, received revelation that he was to restore the Old Testament practice of polygamy. Although his first plural union may have occurred in the mid-1830s, it was not until the early 1840s that he introduced the principle of plural marriage in a more official capacity to a small, trusted circle of Latter-day Saints in Nauvoo, Illinois.

In Nauvoo, plural marriage remained secret; participants made eternal marriage covenants, but few publicly acknowledged them. In contrast, a decade later in the Mountain West, polygamy was preached from the pulpit and lived openly by hundreds, and later thousands, of Saints, although the majority of Church members were monogamous. In the 1880s, the practice again went underground due to heavily enforced federal antipolygamy legislation. In 1890, Church President Wilford Woodruff issued a Manifesto that initiated the end of the practice of polygamy within the Church. A small number of plural marriages did occur thereafter as Latter-day Saints transitioned to monogamy, the only marital arrangement approved of by The Church of Jesus Christ of Latter-day Saints today.

Many modern Latter-day Saints have questions about the Church's polygamous history and want to understand it better. Why did Latter-day Saints embrace plural marriage? How was it practiced? How does it apply to Church members today and in the future? This book aims to address these questions in a concise and accessible way, telling the story of polygamy from the perspective of those who practiced it.

To help simplify the complicated history of polygamy, this book is grounded in five key elements, or five "puzzle pieces," that together help to create a more well-rounded picture of plural marriage. These five interlocking pieces have shaped the content and focus of this book:

1. Theology, or the religious beliefs of Latter-day Saints
2. Historical context, explaining the external circumstances that affected the Saints' opportunities and choices

3. Strong historical sources, using original, primary records whenever possible
4. Stories from polygamous individuals and their children, representing the realities of lived polygamy
5. Religious faith, illustrating the spiritual convictions that influenced Latter-day Saints

While studying a single puzzle piece may satisfy the need some have to understand polygamy, we cannot look at one puzzle piece and think we see the entire picture of plural marriage. Rather, our clarity expands by putting together these puzzle pieces and seeing the larger—although still imperfect—portrait they collectively create.

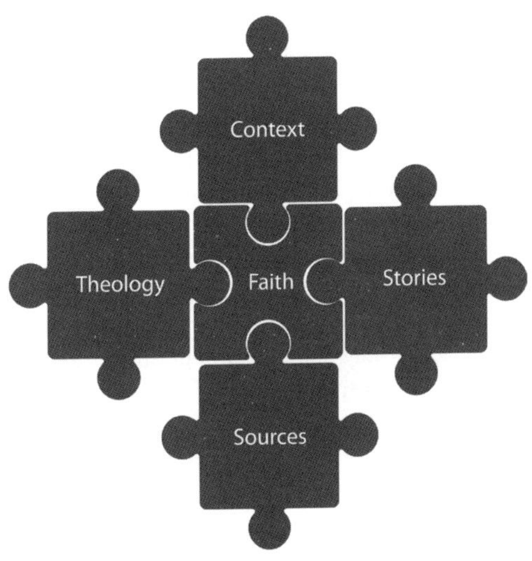

Organization

Aspects of these five puzzle pieces are interwoven throughout each of the three sections in this volume. The first section is a basic chronological history of plural marriage, highlighting changes in the practice over time. The second section explores how and why Latter-day Saints practiced plural marriage. The third section gives voice to a breadth of individual Latter-day Saints and their families as they tell their own stories in their own words.

Lastly, the conclusion of the book addresses the question "What does polygamy mean for Latter-day Saints today?" It looks at the lasting effects of the practice of plural marriage and what modern Latter-day Saints can understand about themselves and their place in history, both now and in the future.

Because this book is a short introduction to plural marriage, not all questions will be answered here. Readers are encouraged to consult the Further Reading section at the end of this book for a list of reliable sources, from the Church as well as scholars, that address specific topics in greater detail. The endnotes will also point readers to a rich array of additional sources to consult.

This book intends to tell the story of polygamy from the perspective of nineteenth-century Latter-day Saints. For most Saints, practicing polygamy was an act of faith. Religious faith is perhaps the most important piece of the overall puzzle that is polygamy. Faith is the inexplicable, critical element that animates theology, brings light to historical context, gives depth to historical sources, and is the connecting thread that unites the stories of Latter-day Saints. Without faith in the restored gospel of Jesus Christ, the practice of plural marriage would not have taken root. Although our understanding of polygamy may never be perfect, respecting the early Saints' faith in this principle gives grace to the whole picture.

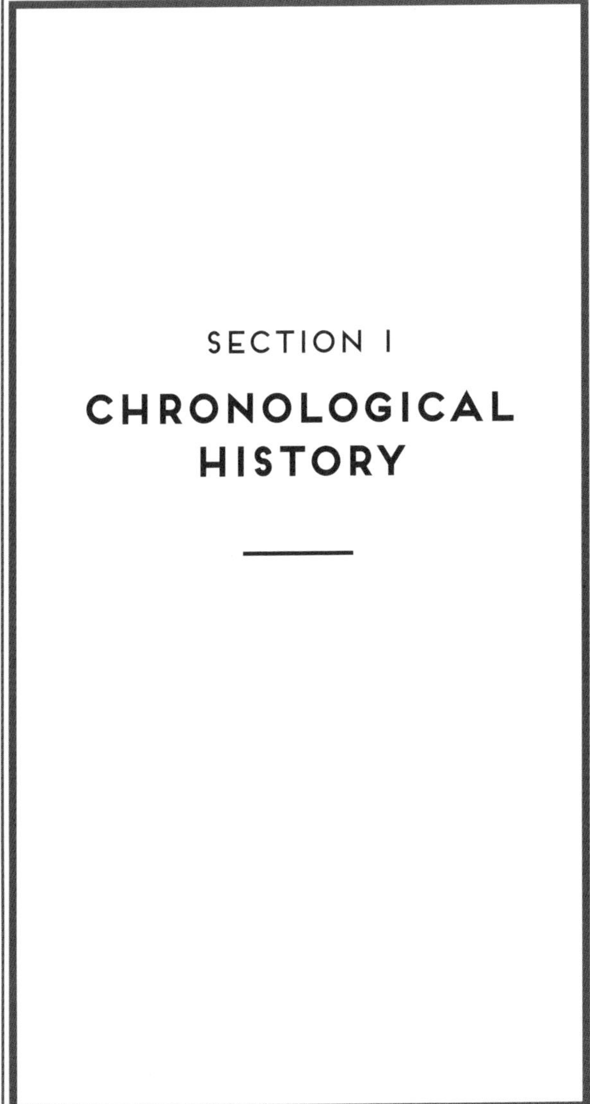

SECTION I

CHRONOLOGICAL HISTORY

CHAPTER 1

BEGINNINGS OF POLYGAMY (1830–40)

"Marriage [is] an institution of heaven."
—Joseph Smith, 1835

The story of polygamy in The Church of Jesus Christ of Latter-day Saints began when Joseph Smith declared that the heavens were opened and God was again speaking to His children, raining down revelations upon His newly formed Church. This restored church was patterned after Christ's ancient design, with prophets and apostles, organized under divine priesthood authority. The establishment of the Church promised to bring forth a restoration of all things preparatory to the Second Coming of Christ, ushering in a new heaven and a new earth.

When Joseph Smith organized the Church in 1830, its theology was still evolving. Continuing revelation guided the development of doctrine "line upon line, precept upon precept" as Joseph asked God questions and received revelatory answers (2 Ne. 28:30). Principles that would later become central to the Latter-day Saint faith, such as temple ordinances and eternal families, were still in embryo, and the Saints' understanding of them would mature with the Church.

Latter-day Saint Views on Marriage, 1830–35

When the Church was founded, Latter-day Saint beliefs about marriage were likely indistinguishable from those of other Christian faiths. The Saints held that marriage was "ordained of God," and they embraced New Testament teachings affirming love and oneness in monogamous marriage (see D&C 42:22–26; 49:15–17; 101 [1835 ed.]). The early Saints largely adhered to traditional laws and cultural practices that placed men at the head of the family as well as society (see Gen. 3:16–17; Eph. 5:22–23). Although traditional marriage and social roles were being challenged by some groups, the early Saints accepted mainstream ideology that monogamous marriage was central to a moral society.[1] Joseph Smith and his wife, Emma Hale, were married in 1827, and they developed a partnership of mutual respect, deep friendship, and shared faith.[2]

Early Revelations on Marriage, 1831

While Latter-day Saints largely adhered to the conventional view of marriage, they began to develop a unique perception of the doctrine as early as 1831, when Joseph Smith "inquired of the Lord" for "a more perfect understanding" of marriage at the urging of convert Leman Copley, previously a celibate Shaker.[3] Joseph's resulting revelation endowed marriage with eternal creative purpose and established matrimony as essential to God's eternal plan for humankind (see D&C 49:15–17). The first intimation of the Saints' eventual practice of plural marriage may have occurred that same year, when Joseph worked on an inspired translation of the Bible. While so doing, he pondered the significance of polygamy as practiced by Abraham and other ancient patriarchs and received revelation from the Lord that polygamy would be reinstituted in the future but "that the time had not come to teach or practice it."[4]

The doctrines of eternal marriage and plural marriage would, years later, develop into a symphony of family-centered theology in which family ties endured forever, beyond this mortal life. Although the concepts of eternal marriage and plural marriage unfolded around the same time, they were—and remain—distinct ideas.[5] Eternal marriage is the foundational doctrine upon which plural marriage was built, but eternal marriage exists independently of plural marriage in the form of monogamy, making plural marriage only a component of the larger, more comprehensive principle of eternal marriage.

Development of Eternal Marriage Doctrine

The nature of marriage continued to be a subject of inquiry for Joseph Smith, even as the Saints endured persecution in Ohio and Missouri. Latter-day Saint doctrine further diverged from other Christian faiths as the Prophet's understanding of eternal marriage and plural marriage matured.

Joseph alluded to elements of the developing doctrine of eternal marriage while performing his first civil marriage on November 24, 1835, uniting Lydia Goldthwaite Bailey with Newel Knight. During the ceremony, Joseph described marriage as "an institution of heaven," teaching that marriage was not just a civil contract and earthly condition but rather a religious covenant and heavenly condition. Joseph then solemnized the couple's union "by the authority of the everlasting priesthood," clarifying that priesthood power given from God, not authority given from civil institutions, bound families together.[6]

The First Plural Marriage, mid-1830s

Fragmentary sources suggest that in the mid-1830s Joseph introduced the principle of plural marriage to Latter-day Saint relatives of Fanny Alger, a Church member who worked in the Smith home in Kirtland, Ohio. Joseph received permission from Fanny's parents to marry their daughter, and with the knowledge of several of her family members, Fanny consented to marry Joseph as a plural wife.[7] Little is known about their union. No firsthand accounts of their marriage exist, and information has been gleaned only from several second- and third-hand sources with varying degrees of reliability. It is uncertain how much Emma knew of Joseph and Fanny's relationship. In 1836, Fanny and her family moved from Ohio, and Fanny married Solomon Custer in Indiana shortly thereafter.[8] Fanny's parents eventually rejoined the main body of

Saints, and Joseph seems to have set aside the doctrine of plural marriage for several years.

Sealing Power, 1836–40

In April 1836, Joseph Smith received priesthood keys, or divine authority, from the ancient prophet Elijah to seal in heaven ordinances performed on earth, giving rise to the term "sealing" to refer to solemnizing eternal marriage and family relationships (see D&C 110:13–16).[9] With the sealing power, Joseph now had formal authority to transition marriage from a temporal institution in which "death us do part" to an eternal ordinance, in which a couple was bound, or sealed, in the eternities.[10] Based on available sources, Joseph did not teach publicly about this visitation, but later sermons indicate that it shaped his understanding of marriage and family relationships in the hereafter.[11]

The Familial Order of Heaven

Joseph Smith gradually introduced the doctrine of eternal marriage to select associates. In the winter of 1840, Joseph Smith taught Apostle Parley P. Pratt that he could remain with his wife "for time and all eternity" and that their posterity could increase even after death. Parley rejoiced; his view of heaven transformed from a place "weaned" of family affection to a paradise filled with loved ones. The promise that family relationships could have divine permanence brought great happiness and peace to the small number of Saints to whom Joseph taught this early doctrine. Parley later reflected, though, that Joseph "had merely lifted a corner of the veil and given me a single glance into eternity." Parley had learned of marriage's eternity, but not yet of its potential plurality.[12]

Eventually, Joseph Smith's revelations about marriage would place the sealing ordinance at the core of exaltation, eternally uniting the Saints together with generations untold, making family the foundation of heavenly life.

CHAPTER 2

NAUVOO POLYGAMY (1841–46)

"My God! thou knowest my integrity.
Be thou my judge I pray thee."
—*Mary Fielding Smith, ca. 1843*

As Latter-day Saints gathered in Nauvoo, Illinois, theology surrounding the eternal nature of the family began to solidify. It had been developing for nearly a decade alongside revelation introducing the organization of the priesthood, the sealing power, and ordinances for the dead. Joseph's early teachings about eternal marriage had been well received, and he felt an urgency to introduce and implement plural marriage and other temple ordinances because God had commanded him to do so, and he knew his life could be cut short at any time.[1] Joseph understood that polygamy would be extremely controversial and that introducing it was a radical, even dangerous, undertaking.

Thus, Joseph introduced the practice of polygamy secretly and gradually in Nauvoo between 1841 and 1844, quietly building support for the practice among close, trusted Church members. He proceeded with caution for several reasons. Western society was generally repulsed by polygamy; it countered traditional marriage vows, defied family norms, and seemed to violate God's commandments.[2] Joseph understood that the practice could repel Church members and inflame already fragile relations with the Saints' neighbors. Moreover, he knew that his wife, Emma, struggled mightily with the principle, and he faced excruciating choices about how to proceed without her full support.

Because Joseph preached the principle secretly and participants held the practice as sacred, few kept records of plural marriage during this period. For this reason, there is much we do not and cannot know about plural marriage in Nauvoo, but credible sources provide enough information to piece together a fundamental account of how it developed.[3]

Development of Plural Marriage in Nauvoo, 1841–43

The men and women to whom Joseph Smith first taught the principle of plural marriage saw Joseph as a prophet of God. Some immediately believed the doctrine, but retrospective accounts indicate that most initially resisted entering the unconventional marriage practice.[4] Joseph Smith's first polygamous marriage in Nauvoo occurred in April 1841 when he was sealed to twenty-six-year-old Louisa Beaman. Over the next three years, he was sealed to additional women, a number of whom were legally married to other men.[5] Joseph was the only documented Latter-day Saint polygamist until June 1842, when Lucy Ann Decker was sealed to Brigham Young.[6] The practice began gaining momentum among others thereafter.

In earnest discipleship, many, like Hyrum Smith's wife Mary Fielding Smith, married or consented for their husbands to marry polygamously solely because they believed plural marriage was a commandment from God. Demonstrating her intense inner struggle over the practice, Mary wrote, "My God! thou knowest my integrity. Be thou my judge I pray thee."[7] Others were unsupportive of the practice. Joseph Smith's first counselor, William Law, for example, was adamantly opposed to polygamy and eventually left the Church. Joseph's clerk William Clayton felt differently; he is the only person known to have kept a detailed, contemporary account of Nauvoo polygamy and wrote in 1843 that marrying polygamously was "a favor which I have long desired."[8]

Joseph Smith's Practice of Plural Marriage

Through the Restoration, Joseph Smith introduced an expansive vision of heaven where, by ordinances and covenants, each person is connected in a vast network of relationships through the sealing ordinance. During the Nauvoo period, these connections were not just vertical links welding ancestor to progeny; they were horizontal as well, as friends were sometimes sealed to friends or mentors in "adoptive" relationships, linking families and friends together eternally.[9] Benjamin F. Johnson, Joseph's intimate friend and fellow Nauvoo polygamist, wrote that "the Prophet taught us . . . that our great mission to Earth was to Organize a Neculi [nuclei] of Heaven to take with us."[10] Using the sealing power, Joseph may have been creating "a network of related wives, children, and kinsmen that would endure into the eternities," because, "like Abraham of old, Joseph yearned for familial plentitude" and the eternal blessings he believed the sealing ordinance would bring for all.[11]

Most scholars estimate that Joseph Smith was sealed to between thirty and forty women.[12] About twenty women left behind personal records attesting that they had been plural wives to Joseph Smith, although the number and strength of corroborating records varies. Compelling secondhand sources from family members and close friends identify about ten additional women, but the women themselves left no records making that claim. Several other women have been named as plural wives based on more distant sources. Because scholars interpret existing historical data differently, an exact number has not been agreed upon.

The majority of women to whom Joseph Smith was sealed were between the ages of twenty and forty.[13] The oldest woman he married was fifty-eight-year-old Rhoda Richards, sister to Apostle Willard Richards. The youngest was fourteen-year-old Helen Mar Kimball, daughter of Apostle Heber C. Kimball. Both of these sealings were likely motivated by the desire to link together two close families. Helen was introduced to the doctrine of plural marriage by her father, who, she wrote, had a "great desire to be connected with the Prophet, Joseph." Believing that her marriage would "ensure [her] eternal salvation and exaltation & that of [her] father's household & all of [her] kindred," Helen wrote, "I willingly gave myself to purchase so glorious a reward."[14]

It was sometimes taught that men who were ordained to priesthood office or who held prominent Church leadership positions were the more desirable persons to whom to be sealed. For that reason, many women and men desired to connect themselves to Joseph Smith through sealing. Church members anticipated that by being sealed to prominent men—either through adoption or marriage—they would inherit eternal blessings in the next life (at the same time, however, faithful men who did not hold prominent positions also married plural wives).[15]

Records suggest Joseph Smith did not woo or court any of the women he married plurally. According to existing accounts, before Joseph proposed a sealing, he often first requested permission from a woman's male relative or her parent(s), and they served as intermediaries on his behalf. This pattern was common for monogamous marriages at the time as well, and in the case of plural marriages, using an intermediary also likely helped to promote trust and confidentiality.

Sometimes Joseph approached women directly. When Joseph asked Lucy Walker to be his plural wife, she recalled feeling "indignant and so expressed myself to him." Lucy was assured by Joseph that she "was entitled to receive a testimony of [plural marriage's] divine origin for [herself]." Lucy wrote, "He counselled me to pray to the Lord, which I did, and thereupon received from [H]im a powerful and irresistible testimony of the truthfulness and divinity of plural marriage, which testimony has abided with me ever since."[16] She and Joseph were sealed in 1843.

The women to whom Joseph Smith was sealed each had strong ties to the Church and to Joseph Smith, either through their longevity in the Church or through male relatives who held prominent leadership positions. None were new converts or new to Nauvoo, and, whether by connection or inclination, many of these women were or became strong female leaders in the Church.[17]

Joseph seems to have consistently advised prospective wives to seek their own witness of the principle. He likewise counseled men to whom he taught the principle to receive their own testimonies. At no time did Joseph Smith perform his own marriage ceremonies. Based on the few descriptions we have of his sealing ceremonies, they were performed in private by someone with priesthood authority in the presence of at least one male or female witness.[18]

Plural Marriage and Physical Intimacy

Whether a plural marriage included intimacy depended on the marriage. Plural sealings in Nauvoo were conducted for time and eternity or for eternity alone. Couples sealed *only* for eternity were not considered married in mortality and did not have sexual relations. Marriages for *time* and eternity, however, could include physical intimacy. Joseph was sealed to some of his wives for time and eternity and others for eternity alone, although the number of each is not known due to a lack of records. Emily Partridge and Malissa Lott, two wives to whom Joseph was sealed for time and eternity, testified under oath that their marriages did include sexual relations. Later first- and secondhand accounts suggest the same was true in at least some of his other marriages. Other plural marriages, however, probably did not include physical intimacy.[19] Joseph's youngest wife, Helen, emphasized that her sealing was for "eternity alone," suggesting that her marriage was not consummated.[20]

Although Joseph and Emma Smith had nine biological children, there is no solid evidence to date—including from genetic testing—that Joseph Smith had children with any of his plural wives.[21] When Malissa Lott was questioned as to why she thought there was no progeny, she responded, "Through no fault of either of us, lack of proper conditions on my part probably, or it might be in the wisdom of the Almighty that we should have none."[22]

Joseph Smith and Polyandry

One puzzling attribute of Joseph Smith's practice of polygamy was that he was sealed to women who were already married to living men, a practice sometimes called polyandry. Indeed, of Joseph's first twelve plural sealings, nine were to women who were legally married.[23] Virtually all of the married women continued to live and have children with their legal husbands after their marriages to Joseph. These plural marriages may have been for eternity alone because no reliable sources have been found that confirm sexual relations.[24] Joseph Smith is the only person known to have engaged in polyandrous sealings.

Little is known about the nature or purpose of these polyandrous sealings. According to reminiscent accounts, Joseph hesitated to introduce plural marriage until a sword-bearing angel threatened his life and the progress of the Church if he did not go forward.[25] During his period of hesitation, Joseph had been prompted to marry specific women who were then single, but he did not act upon those promptings. When Joseph instituted plural marriage some time later, several of those women had already married. Despite this, Joseph evidently believed that he was still obligated to be sealed to those specific women, and they agreed to be sealed.[26]

Twenty-year-old Zina Huntington was newly married to Henry Jacobs when Joseph Smith renewed a sealing proposal she had rejected prior to her marriage. Decades later, she recounted, "I obtained a testimony for myself that God had required that order to be established in his church," and, with the support of her husband, Henry, Zina made what she felt was "a greater sacrifise than to give my life" in choosing to be sealed to Joseph in October 1841.[27] She continued to live with Henry and bore him two children before she and Henry separated. Zina married Brigham Young for time and became an influential leader in the Relief Society.[28]

Scholars have suggested additional explanations as to why polyandrous sealings occurred. Some may have been "horizontal" sealings intended to create eternal bonds between families in an impulse similar to Heber C. Kimball's wish to be linked with the Smith family in the hereafter. Also, several of the legally married women to whom Joseph was sealed had husbands who were not Church members or were disaffected members. Those women may have wanted to secure eternal blessings through their union with Joseph.[29]

Scandal in Nauvoo

In the spring of 1842, Nauvoo became embroiled in scandal. John C. Bennett, an opportunist who had quickly risen to civic and religious prominence, was accused of seducing women by practicing "spiritual wifery" under the guise of Church approval.[30] Spiritual wifery was "little more than illicit sexual relations kept secret"—a perverted perception of what Joseph Smith called celestial marriage.[31] After John C. Bennett was exposed in May 1842, he was excommunicated and left Nauvoo. John then turned accusations of sexual misconduct against Joseph Smith and published his allegations, with those of several other disaffected Church members, in a book-length exposé that confused some Saints and aroused bitter anti-Mormon sentiment.[32]

Rumors, amplified by John C. Bennett's allegations, prompted Joseph Smith and others to offer "carefully worded denials" to charges of polygamy based upon their redefined understanding of marriage.[33] To Joseph and other practitioners, eternal marriage, including plural marriage, was an order of the priesthood, a spiritual covenant that was different from civil marriage (see D&C 131:1–4; 22:1–4). Thus, because polygamous men claimed no *legal* wives aside from their first, some felt justified in saying they had only one wife. Others denied practicing polygamy in the sense associated with the harems in Asia and the Middle East. They considered celestial marriage to be a system of matrimony entirely separate from other marriage systems and referred to it with a variety of euphemisms.[34] Eliza R. Snow, a plural wife of Joseph Smith, felt justified signing a public statement in 1842 that denied the existence of a "secret wife system" in the Church because, she wrote, "There [was] no reference to divine plural marriage [in the document]."[35] With that rationale, she felt she could sign honestly.

Were polygamous Saints, including Joseph Smith, lying in making these denials? Some Saints certainly felt deceived, and the approach chosen by early polygamists may be disconcerting. In their view, however, God had commanded them to institute plural marriage, and keeping it secret by delicately mincing words seemed necessary for the growth of polygamy and the safety of the Saints. They differentiated the definitions of civil and celestial marriage so firmly that they, at least, felt they were telling the truth.

The commandment to the general Church was, at that time, to live monogamously *except* for those specifically called to practice polygamy by Joseph Smith. Thus, even as Joseph Smith and others fulfilled the Lord's command to marry plurally, Joseph continued to publicly preach the Lord's usual standard that "no man shall have but one wife."[36]

Joseph, Emma, and Plural Marriage

Throughout this tumultuous period, Joseph felt support from his first wife, Emma. In 1842, in the thick of the John C. Bennett scandal, Joseph referred to her as his "undaunted, firm and unwavering, unchangeable, affectionate Emma."[37] They closed letters to each other with sentiments of love.[38] During a serious illness Emma contracted in the fall of 1842, Joseph stayed by her bedside and cared for her. Emma was devoted to her husband, and he to her.

It is unclear how much Emma knew about her husband's practice of polygamy at this point. Emma's personal experience of polygamy is largely preserved like Joseph's—through the diaries and reminiscences of others. Firsthand sources documenting her experience of plural marriage do not exist beyond an interview published after her death in which she denied

Courtesy Community of Christ Archives, Independence, MO.

Emma Smith in 1845 with her son David Hyrum, with whom she was pregnant when Joseph was martyred in 1844.

that Joseph practiced polygamy.[39] Thus, her inner story, the inner workings of her relationship with Joseph, and the extent of her knowledge, understanding, and approval of polygamy is not definitively known.

Putting together the fragments of her story, we learn that by the spring of 1843, Emma knew with certainty that Joseph practiced plural marriage. She was also aware of some of the women to whom he was sealed. Emma was not aware, however, of all of his sealings. She accepted the doctrine of plural marriage around this time and consented to and attended at least four ceremonies in which Joseph was sealed to other women.[40] Emma and Joseph were then sealed on May 28, 1843. Emma vacillated in her support of polygamy. Four women to whom she knew Joseph was sealed lived in the Smith home as household help, and the situation soon soured for Emma. Joseph's plural wife Emily Dow Partridge recalled that shortly after Emma permitted Joseph to be sealed to Emily and Emily's sister Eliza, Emma instructed them to renounce their vows and leave the Smith home. The Partridge sisters left the home but refused to renounce their vows.[41] By July 1843, plural marriage had become an intense point of conflict in Emma's relationship with Joseph.[42]

The Eternal Marriage and Plural Marriage Revelation, 1843

Although Joseph Smith may have received instruction about the practice of polygamy as early as 1831, he did not record it. At his brother Hyrum's request, Joseph dictated a revelation on eternal and plural marriage to his scribe William Clayton on July 12, 1843. Emma's resistance to plural marriage provides a backdrop for the text of this revelation.

Three decades later, William related the events of that day as clearly as he could remember. According to William, Hyrum said to Joseph:

> "If you will write the revelation on Celestial marriage, I will take, and read it to Emma, and I believe I can convince her of its truth, and you will hereafter have peace." Joseph smiled, and remarked, "you do not know Emma as well as I do." Hyrum repeated his opinion and further remarked, "the doctrine is so plain I can convince any reasonable man or woman of its truth, purity and heavenly origin," or words to their effect. Joseph then said, "well, I will write the revelation, and we will see."

Joseph proceeded to dictate, keeping in mind his audience—his wife Emma and perhaps a close circle of followers.[43] A portion of the revelation is explicitly addressed to Emma (see D&C 132:51–57).[44]

Hyrum presented Emma with the revelation, and William Clayton recorded in his personal 1843 diary that Emma "said she did not believe a word of it and appeared very rebellious." The couple's tensions over polygamy did not resolve, and one month later, Emma threatened divorce. William recorded in his diary on August 16, 1843, that Emma "resisted the P[rinciple] in toto, and he [Joseph] had to tell her he would relinquish all [his wives] for her sake," knowing that if he did not, Emma would "obtain a divorce and leave him."[45] Joseph confided to William that he would not abandon his wives, but he slowed the practice almost completely for himself, though not for others.

Despite their immense difficulties, Emma and Joseph did reconcile. In February 1844, Emma became pregnant with their ninth child. In June 1844, Emma wrote to Joseph, who was imprisoned in Carthage Jail, "I desire with all my heart to honor and respect my husband as my head, ever to live in his confidence and by acting in unison with him retain the place which God has given me by his side."[46]

After years of reflecting on these incidents, Joseph's plural wife Emily Partridge wrote in 1883, "I can truly say; poor Emma. She could not stand polygamy, but she was a good woman, and I never wish to stand in her way of happiness and exaltation. . . . If the Lord will, my heart says let Emma come and stand in her place. Perhaps she has done no worse than any of us would have done in her place. Let the Lord be the judge."[47]

Regardless of Emma's opposition to the plural marriage revelation, it was read confidentially to other Saints and considered the word of God by those who accepted it. It remained a private document for almost a decade, even as the number of polygamous Church members increased. It was not until 1852 that the revelation was read from the pulpit to reinforce that the principle had been revealed to Joseph Smith. The revelation was published as scripture in the 1876 edition of the Doctrine and Covenants and is now known as Doctrine and Covenants 132.

It matters that Doctrine and Covenants 132 remained a private document and that the revelation was intended, at least in part, for Emma Smith. In 1878, Joseph F. Smith, then a counselor in the First Presidency, stated that the revelation as it was written in 1843 "was not then designed to go forth to the church or to the world. It is most probable that had it been then written with a view to its going out as a doctrine of the church, it would have been presented in a somewhat different form." President Joseph F. Smith suggested that private matters "not relevant to the principle [of plural marriage] itself" were interwoven into the revelation, implying that the personal portions of the document—those perhaps influenced by Emma's opposition to polygamy—might not have been included if the revelation were intended for the general Church membership.[48] Regardless of how the revelation came about and who it was intended for, it was later used to shape and defend the practice of polygamy in the Church as a whole.

Less than one year after the revelation on eternal and plural marriage was recorded, Joseph and Hyrum Smith were martyred at Carthage Jail in Illinois on June 27, 1844. Tensions related to plural marriage in Nauvoo had contributed to Joseph and Hyrum being imprisoned in Carthage after the printing press of the *Nauvoo Expositor*, a paper criticizing the practice of plural marriage, was destroyed. After Joseph's death, Brigham Young and the Quorum of the Twelve Apostles were sustained to lead the Church.[49] By that time, nearly every member of the Twelve had married polygamously. They were converted to the principle of plural marriage and committed to perpetuating, and expanding, the practice.[50] The 1843 revelation was the only written, substantive document detailing the doctrine and served as leaders' foundational guide for how and why to practice polygamy after Joseph's death.

The Plural Widows of Joseph and Hyrum Smith

The martyred Joseph left behind between thirty and forty wives, and Hyrum left three.[51] Following the model of biblical levirate marriages, in which the brother of a deceased man married his widow(s), Church leaders believed it was their responsibility to care for the widows of Joseph and Hyrum. Thus, given the opportunity, about half of Joseph and Hyrum's widows chose to marry members of the Quorum of the Twelve, most electing to wed either Heber C. Kimball or Brigham Young. The other half married other men, remained with their husband if they were already married, or chose not to remarry.[52]

Under the leadership of the Quorum of the Twelve, plural marriage transitioned from a private, spiritual sphere of eternal covenants to a more temporal, earthly practice of creating and supporting families. Some wives began living in their new households and bore children by their new husbands. Others, such as Eliza R. Snow, who married Brigham Young, were not necessarily conjugal wives but instead looked to their husbands as men under covenant to offer economic support and protection.[53]

Increasing Numbers

At the time of Joseph Smith's death, only about twenty-nine men and fifty women had married plurally, not including Joseph and his wives. Most men were sealed to only one additional wife.[54] During the winter of 1845–46, just before the migration west began, hundreds of Latter-day Saints entered into plural marriages and solemnized their unions in the Nauvoo Temple. One scholar estimated that by the end of the Nauvoo period in 1846, 153 men had married 587 women (this number includes first wives).[55] Many monogamous couples were also sealed, demonstrating that early Latter-day Saints saw eternal marriage as independent of plural marriage.[56]

Emma continued to resist the practice of polygamy and remained in Nauvoo with her children and Joseph Smith's mother, Lucy Mack Smith. As Emma's children grew, she taught them of the prophetic calling of their father, the divine authenticity of the Book of Mormon, and her "complete faith" in the restored gospel, but she firmly denied that Joseph practiced polygamy.[57] She supported her eldest son, Joseph Smith III, as president of the Reorganized Church of Jesus Christ of Latter Day Saints (now known as the Community of Christ), established in 1860, a sect that strongly opposed plural marriage.[58] Thus, the story of polygamy faded east of the Mississippi River. For the Saints who crossed the Mississippi and traveled west, the story of polygamy was just beginning.

CHAPTER 3

POLYGAMY IN TRANSITION (1846–47)

"Women; this is my husband's wife!"
—Zina D. H. Young, remembering 1846

While the Saints slogged through the mud of Iowa and established temporary settlements on the banks of the Missouri River, the practicalities of polygamy surfaced. The freedom of the frontier allowed many plural families to live together for the first time. As families transitioned from the private to public practice of polygamy, they confronted the temporal challenges of a polygamous lifestyle, including ambiguities about family relationships and roles. In response, the practice of polygamy became more systematized, answering questions of who practiced plural marriage and how.

Sugar Creek, Iowa, 1846

In 1846, as many as fourteen thousand Latter-day Saints left Nauvoo in forced exodus due to mob violence and lack of protection from the Illinois state government. The Saints looked beyond the borders of the United States to build a peaceful Zion community.[1] In February 1846, the first group of two thousand Saints crossed the Mississippi River to Sugar Creek, Iowa, eight miles from Nauvoo. Zina D. H. Young, a plural wife of first Joseph Smith and then Brigham Young, rejoiced in the freedom of Sugar Creek, remembering, "Here we had now openly the first examples of noble-minded, virtuous women, bravely commencing to live in the newly revealed order of celestial marriage. 'Women; this is my husband's wife!' Here, at length, we could give this introduction, without fear of reproach, or violation of man-made laws."[2]

Despite Zina's feeling of liberation, polygamy was not yet officially acknowledged as a tenet of The Church of Jesus Christ of Latter-day Saints. Church leaders continued to publicly deny the practice and did not sermonize on the topic, but visible plural relationships, coupled with the increased numbers of polygamists sealed in the Nauvoo Temple, brought a hushed awareness of the practice to many in Latter-day Saint communities. Some Latter-day Saints, however—particularly those living outside the United States—were still unaware of the principle.

Polygamy in Iowa and Nebraska, 1846–48

As the nomadic "Camp of Israel" moved slowly across Iowa, it became clear that the Saints needed to stop and prepare for the winter of 1846–47 before continuing west. About forty Latter-day Saint communities dotted Iowa and Nebraska in a matter of months and became home to nearly twelve thousand migrating Saints.[3] Rising from the banks of the Missouri River, Winter Quarters, Nebraska, became Church headquarters and home to 3,483 Latter-day Saints by December 1846.[4]

In these challenging circumstances, plural families tried to adapt to the unfamiliar marriage system. Emmeline B. Woodward was deserted by her first husband in Nauvoo and married Bishop Newel K. Whitney as a plural wife in 1845. Young women like Emmeline, who otherwise would have been alone, benefited from belonging to an established household like that of the Whitneys, who had means to provide for her. Emmeline dearly loved her new family, and her diary is remarkably upbeat given what the Saints experienced during this period—poor housing, insufficient food, widespread illness, and numerous deaths.

Not everyone, however, had a positive experience with the new practice. Patty Sessions recorded months of discord with her husband's new wife, Rosilla, whom he had married in Nauvoo. Now on the frontier, Patty and Rosilla lived together for the first time. As their wagon rolled westward, they clashed over family responsibilities and endured distressing experiences involving intimacy, cruelty, and deceit. Their husband, David, was ill-prepared to handle the new marital dynamic and threatened to abandon his first wife, Patty. At Winter Quarters, David's marriage with Rosilla dissolved, and Rosilla returned to Nauvoo alone.[5]

Just across the river from Winter Quarters, in Council Bluffs, Iowa, Mary Parker Richards wrote to her missionary husband, Samuel. She had witnessed unhappy polygamous unions like the Sessions', so when Samuel suggested by letter that they add a second wife to their family when he returned, Mary objected. She explained, "If you had seen what I have seen you would not wonder why I thus wrote for there is no such thing as happiness known here where a man has more than one [wife]. It realy seems to me that this is a day in which Woman is destined to misery."[6]

Polygamy was hard for families. However, many Saints were willing to endure a great deal before forsaking the covenants they had made in the Nauvoo Temple and the blessings they anticipated receiving here and in the hereafter through their marriage vows. Some polygamous families managed to adapt, but not all plural marriages survived the trek to Utah. Some unions ended in "writing[s] of releasement," and other couples simply walked away from each other.[7]

Challenges during the Transition Period

Regulating the Practice

One pressing trial for Church leaders was regulating plural marriages. The Church was traveling west, and Latter-day Saints were strewn from Nebraska to Missouri. Without keeping a tight rein on who married polygamously, the practice could easily get out of hand. Because polygamy was not openly discussed, Saints were unclear about its rules, leaving it open to abuse. In a private meeting with several male leaders in Winter Quarters, Brigham Young censured men who misled "innocent, ignorant females" and went without permission "to some clod head of an elder" who, without proper authority, conducted the ceremony. "This is not right and will not be suffered," President Young said.[8] Brigham Young followed a pattern set by Joseph Smith in the revelation on eternal marriage—no plural marriage could occur without the permission of the Church President or his designee.[9] President Young further mandated that no plural marriages should occur along the trail west, although a few exceptions were made.[10]

Lack of a Marriage Model

Another practical challenge for first-generation polygamists was that there was no successful marriage model to follow. The nineteenth-century model was monogamy, which implied a physical, financial, and emotional oneness difficult to achieve in polygamy.[11] A husband was expected to lead, protect, and provide for his family; he fathered children and was an intimate counselor to his wife and active presence in family life. A wife was a partner to her husband, bore and mothered children, and ran the household. Although many tried, these monogamous expectations could not be superimposed upon polygamous relationships. The two systems were inherently different. Individuals struggled to define the responsibilities plural husbands and wives had to one another.

Frequently, there was a disconnect between the spiritual ideals and temporal realities of plural marriage. Nancy Bean Williams married John D. Lee as his first plural wife on February 5, 1845, and later gave birth to their daughter, Cordelia. By the time thirty-four-year-old John arrived in Winter Quarters in August 1846, he had ten wives and added four more while there.[12] In January 1847, John recorded that Nancy wrote him a letter from her parents' home, where she had been staying, "counselling [John] to take care of [his] family, having reference to herself." He did not respond, so Nancy wrote again, reminding her husband that she looked to him for "salvation spiritually" as well as temporally, and as John's wife and mother of his child, she wanted to know "what [John's] feelings are, what she might depend on." This spiritual union had temporal expectations. Nancy had fulfilled her expected role as a wife by bearing a child, but she needed clarification about what role John would fill as her husband. In his response to Nancy, John took an authoritarian approach and "set fourth the law of the covenant and priesthood to her," instructing her to live amongst his other wives and he would care for her.[13] Nancy acquiesced but was dissatisfied with the arrangement and desired more from the man she called her husband. Unable to reconcile, the couple divorced in 1848.[14]

Household Hierarchy

Part of creating a working system in plural families was establishing a household hierarchy. Men remained the head of their families, and first wives held a natural authority in their position as "first." Crossing the plains with five other adult females, including her mother-in-law and three future sister wives, Phebe Carter Woodruff, the first wife of Apostle Wilford Woodruff, exerted leadership as the female head of the household. She established a pecking order of sorts based on assignments and responsibilities, and she expected obedience.[15]

When additional wives joined a family, age and marriage order raised questions of familial authority and hierarchy. When Benjamin F. Johnson married his third wife, Clarinda Gleason, on December 1, 1845, his "real family troubles commenced," he wrote. "The third wife was much older than the second and was of broad experience and capability. She was unwilling to be second to the younger, and was not satisfied with her proper place, and there was now discord in the family circle."[16] Domestic space was also a consideration; a wife typically "presided" within her own space, whether that be a tent, a bedroom, or a home.[17]

As Church leaders and families adapted to polygamous living, growing pains forced the Saints to begin establishing rules and expectations around the practice. Trial and error along the trail from Nauvoo to Utah laid the groundwork that helped to sustain the practice of polygamy over the next half-century.

CHAPTER 4

GROWTH OF POLYGAMY IN THE WEST (1847–81)

"The Latter-day Saints have embraced the doctrine of a plurality of wives."
—*Orson Pratt, 1852*

Free of the persecution that had previously inhibited their religious expression, members of The Church of Jesus Christ of Latter-day Saints began building Zion in Utah Territory and other areas of the Mountain West. Plural marriage merged into the social fabric of Latter-day Saint society, and for about thirty years, the Saints practiced polygamy openly. As children born and raised in plural families entered into polygamous unions themselves, plural marriage influenced the customs and convictions of its second generation.

Polygamy in Frontier Utah, 1847–52

By the time the Saints arrived at the Great Basin, polygamy had created a web of strong family relationships. Many Church members, particularly prominent ones, were now directly or indirectly tied to one another through marriage. Latter-day Saints continued to publicly deny their practice of polygamy, but surveyor Howard Stansbury, who was not a Latter-day Saint, wintered in Salt Lake City from 1849 to 1850 and noted: "That polygamy does actually exist among them cannot be concealed from any one of the most ordinary observation, who has spent even a short time in this community." But, he continued, "I have never known any member of the community to avow that he himself had more than one

[wife], although that such was the fact was as well known and understood as any fact could be."[1] This conspicuous contradiction, however, would soon change.

Announcement, 1852

On Sunday, August 29, 1852, before an audience of about three thousand people, Apostle Orson Pratt publicly announced that The Church of Jesus Christ of Latter-day Saints "embraced the doctrine of a plurality of wives, as a part of their religious faith."[2] With the long silence on plural marriage over, the principle was now official doctrine to be defended, taught, and lived unapologetically. Elder Pratt's statement came as no surprise to Saints in Utah, but he acknowledged members would "have to break up new ground" in parts of the world where they had not preached plural marriage.[3]

The news profoundly affected Church members, missionary work, and the popular perception of Latter-day Saints worldwide. Missionary Richard Ballantyne wrote to his wife from Madras, India, in 1852: "the great bone that is now being picked is Polygamy. This is a large pill for many to swallow, and in fact the very first sight of it so nauseates their stomachs, that at present they can scarcely recieve anything else."[4]

Fanny Stenhouse was on a mission with her husband, Thomas, in Switzerland when the principle was announced. She went to her room to read Joseph Smith's revelation privately. "Before I had got through one half I threw it aside, feeling altogether rebellious against God," she wrote. "I now began to feel perfectly reckless, and even willing to throw aside my religion, and take 'my chance of salvation,' rather than submit to Polygamy; for I felt that that new doctrine was a degradation to womankind."[5] Fanny later allowed her husband to marry plurally, but eventually both Fanny and Thomas left the Church and became strident antipolygamists.

For others, polygamy confirmed their faith in the Church or, as in the case of Emily B. Spencer, inspired conversion. "When eighteen, the revelation on Celestial [Plural] Marriage had just been published. I read it, and my mind being already prepared,

I readily believed it," she wrote. "I clearly saw that if I did not join the Church of Jesus Christ of Latter-day Saints I could not be united with my husband through eternity, as I had fondly hoped. . . . I believed then, as I know now, that this revelation on Celestial Mariage was from the Lord, and I have been blessed in believing it."[6] She and her husband, George, were baptized in October 1852, and George married two additional wives.[7]

Reformation, 1856–57

After nearly ten years in the security of their new settlements, Church leaders believed that the Saints had grown spiritually complacent and needed stoking by "the fire of the Spirit."[8] Thus, the Latter-day Saint Reformation began, peaking between the fall of 1856 and the winter of 1857.[9] During the Reformation period, Church leaders preached fiery sermons emphasizing personal repentance and renewed religious commitment. Masses of Church members were rebaptized to symbolically rededicate themselves to their covenants. For some Saints, reason gave way to militant frenzy, and Hannah Tapfield King remembered the Reformation as "a fearful time for all."[10] Plural marriage was heavily preached in local meetings, and messages of reform were reinforced by "home missionaries," including those filled with more zeal than doctrinal understanding.

In a letter to Brigham Young, Joseph Cluff of Provo wrote that in his area, people were promoting polygamy by teaching that "if an Oald Man should ask a girl to have him, if he was a good man, and she should refuse him she would be Damnd." Thus, a young woman would be "scared into" plural marriage and "take the first that came along whither she wanted him or not." They "soon after got sick of their bargin and left their husbands . . . [and] want a divorse."[11] Church leaders quickly attempted to curb errors. Heber C. Kimball of the First Presidency wrote to James C. Snow, president of the Provo Stake, saying, "We do not wish this matter [plural marriage] forced" and urged him to "use your influence to stop this sort of preaching."[12]

That message did not ring in all ears, however. Emma

Lynne Richardson was among the young women who married during the Reformation. She recalled, "Some old fanatics were preaching that a young man could not save a girl if he married her. That to be saved she must marry some old codger tried and true. My parents got the disease with the rest and when one of the tried and true came our way [they said] I MUST marry him. I cried and begged, begged and cried, but to no avail. I was forced to marry him and go into his family." Thus, at age fourteen, Emma married sixty-one-year-old Freeborn DeMille in 1856. Two children and about four years later, the couple separated, and she later married a man her age. Emma attributed the painful experience to "the pressure of the times."[13]

The number of plural marriages reached its peak in Utah between 1855 and 1857. In Emma's community of Manti, over 40 percent of its population in 1860 belonged to a polygamous family, either as a husband, wife, or child. Historian Kathryn Daynes determined that 38.5 percent of plural marriages that occurred in Manti during the Reformation ended in divorce, a significantly higher proportion than polygamous marriages that occurred before or after.[14]

The hysteria of the Reformation, with its mismatched spousal ages and fear-motivated marriages, negatively affected plural marriage and its image for many years. These disturbing experiences were less common outside of the Reformation period, but they still occurred and are evidence that polygamy was vulnerable to abuse when misunderstood or misused. Having observed plural marriage from its beginnings in Nauvoo to 1875, when she wrote her autobiography, Sarah Sturtevant Leavitt concluded, "I have seen so much wrong connected with this ordinance that had I not had it revealed to me from Him that cannot lie, I should sometimes have doubted the truth of it, but there has never a doubt crossed my mind concerning the truth of it since the Lord made it known to me by a heavenly vision."[15] Sarah's voice joined those who still supported plural marriage in precept, attributing abuses to individual choices, not to the principle itself.

CHAPTER 5

THE ANTIPOLYGAMY CRUSADE (1882–90)

"We leave [Senator Edmunds] and all those who seek to oppress us, in the hands of that God whose laws we have enlisted to obey."

—*Zina D. H. Young, 1883*[1]

When Latter-day Saints publicly preached polygamy in 1852, there were no federal laws in the territorial United States preventing the practice, and Utah's territorial legislature was working toward Utah's becoming a state in the Union. As westward expansion and the transcontinental railroad gradually ended Utah's isolation, the nation became fixed on eradicating polygamy. In fact, the 1856 Republican presidential platform vowed to prohibit "those twin relics of barbarism—Polygamy and Slavery."[2] Public opposition to polygamy prompted the US government to pass a series of laws against the practice, simultaneously squelching the Saints' hopes that Utah would soon become a state. The Church vigorously challenged the constitutionality of the legislation, maintaining that plural marriage was a religious belief and therefore protected by the First Amendment to the US Constitution. In *Reynolds v. United States* (1879), however, the US Supreme Court upheld antipolygamy laws as constitutional, stating that while "religious belief was protected by law, religious practice was not."[3]

Laws Designed to End Polygamy

Morrill Anti-Bigamy Act, 1862

Abraham Lincoln signed into law the Morrill Anti-Bigamy Act, the first piece of legislation targeting polygamy. The Morrill Act made bigamy (marriage to more than one person) illegal in all US territories, overturned the incorporation of the Church granted by the Utah territorial legislature, and restricted ownership of Church property. Because the United States was in the midst of the Civil War, Lincoln chose not to enforce the Morrill Act. There was an unspoken agreement that if Utah stayed out of the Civil War, the federal government would leave the Saints in peace for the time being.[4]

Cullom Bill, 1870

The Cullom Bill passed in the US House of Representatives but failed in the Senate. If it had passed, the bill would have denied US citizenship to those "living in or practicing bigamy, polygamy, or concubinage." Those practicing plural marriage would not have been able to vote, hold public office, or benefit from homesteading laws.[5]

Poland Act, 1874

The Poland Act gave US district courts in Utah full jurisdiction over criminal and civil cases and prevented polygamists from serving on juries. This law gave greater leverage to those attempting to prosecute polygamists.

The Edmunds and Edmunds-Tucker Acts, 1882, 1887

The largely unenforced Morrill Anti-Bigamy Act of 1862 was given teeth in 1882 when the Edmunds Act became law. The Edmunds Act made polygamy a felony and cohabitation a crime punishable by a fine,

Courtesy Church History Library, The Church of Jesus Christ of Latter-day Saints, Salt Lake City

Polygamists in the Utah Penitentiary, 1889

imprisonment, or both. It wrested political power from polygamists and revoked their right to vote, serve on juries, and hold public office. The Edmunds-Tucker Act of 1887 dissolved anything that gave social or political power to the Church or its support of polygamous unions. To decrease Latter-day Saints' political voice, it repealed Utah women's suffrage, a right women had exercised since 1870. The Edmunds-Tucker Act reinforced the Morrill Act's disincorporation of the Church and allowed the federal government to seize any Church property valued over $50,000, thus threatening the confiscation of temples and other Church buildings. The Edmunds and Edmunds-Tucker Acts severely affected families and crippled the Church's ability to function.[6]

Polygamy and Women's Rights Activism, 1870s

As the federal government increased its efforts to end polygamy in the 1870s, the individual and collective achievements of Latter-day Saint women blossomed. They advanced in educational and professional pursuits, engaged in social reform, and organized Church auxiliaries. The Relief Society, which had disbanded before the Saints left Nauvoo, was gradually reestablished in wards.[7]

The 1870 Cullom Bill, then being considered in the US Congress, roused Latter-day Saint women to cooperative action for the first time. "There is a point at which silence is no longer a virtue," declared Eliza R. Snow. "Were we the stupid, degraded, heartbroken beings that we have been represented, silence might better become us; but, as women of God, . . . we not only speak because we have the right, but justice and humanity demand that we should."[8]

Women organized a "Great Indignation Meeting," held on January 13, 1870, in which they boldly defended their right to practice polygamy. Five thousand women crowded the Salt Lake Tabernacle, and all men were banned from the building except reporters. One from the *New York Herald* wrote that the gathering was "one of the grandest female assemblages in all history" and testified that "Mormon women have both brains and tongues."[9] With a voice loud enough to be heard in Congress, their efforts were successful, and the Cullom Bill did not pass the Senate.

Women's defense of polygamy empowered and unified them and set them on a course to advocate for broader women's rights. In February 1870, the Utah territorial legislature gave Utah women the right to vote, making them the second body of women in the nation to be enfranchised, after women in Wyoming, and the first to cast a ballot.[10] In 1872, the influential Latter-day Saint women's newspaper called the *Woman's Exponent* was first printed and reinforced the unity of women Churchwide.

Latter-day Saint women became significantly involved in national and international women's movements and social causes and formed alliances with important leaders. Their acceptance in these circles remained mixed, however. People could not reconcile how women in such a seemingly barbaric

Courtesy Church History Library

Susan B. Anthony (seated at center) with women's suffrage activists in Utah, many of whom belonged to polygamous families, 1895

marriage system could engage in such progressive activities. In 1879, Zina Young Williams and Emmeline B. Wells attended the National Woman Suffrage Association convention in Washington, DC. Both were polygamous wives and became objects of public curiosity. "Dear me," Zina recorded in her diary, "what an awful thing to be an Elephant. The ladies all look at me so queer."[11] Their activism ultimately bore dividends, though, and gave them voice and representation in important causes.

Latter-day Saints took pride in the legal and political advancement of women in Utah Territory. Utah created comparatively liberal laws, in part to allow polygamous households to function. Women could own property, find gainful employment, divorce easily, and vote. Women were also allowed to attend institutions of higher education—something unheard of in other areas of the United States. These egalitarian practices ran counter to what many were convinced was women's repressed condition in Utah.

The Raid and the Underground, 1882–90

Antipolygamy legislation reflected the general assumption that Latter-day Saint women were victims rather than free agents in the plural marriage system and thus specifically targeted men. The Edmunds Act impending, President John Taylor declared his intention to "abide by the laws of God" and continue to practice plural marriage, "risk[ing] the consequences let them be what they may."[12] Many Saints followed their prophet-president and violated federal law by continuing to live polygamously.

The Edmunds and Edmunds-Tucker Acts allowed prosecution for "unlawful cohabitation," and because *cohabitation* was not clearly defined, prosecutors needed only to prove that a man shared a connubial domestic relationship with more than one woman, not that multiple marriage ceremonies had occurred.[13] Law enforcement would commonly arrest a "cohab" by catching him at home with his families or at the home of a plural wife. The ensuing dance between deputy and polygamist led to what has been called "the greatest game of hide-and-seek ever played," though it came with serious consequences.[14]

Between 1882 and 1890, federal deputies poured into Utah, raiding homes to arrest polygamous husbands. This period of harsh and effective enforcement of antipolygamy laws was known as "the Raid." Monetary rewards were offered for information leading to the arrest of polygamists, and Latter-day Saints asserted that "notoriously disreputable characters were employed to spy into men's family relations" and bribe neighbors for information.[15] Strangers were viewed with suspicion, and one plural wife was wary even of other Church members, remembering, "There was no one you could trust in them days."[16] By 1890, every Utah settlement had been searched and searched again, leading to over one thousand arrests.[17]

In his diary, polygamist George Kirkham, husband to Sara and Mary, recorded his own arrest in the early morning of

December 8, 1886: "There was a knock on the door. I arose, went to the door and a boy said the marshal had arrested Bishop Cutler and John Gibbs. I had only got my pants on, when another knock came to the door. I opened the door and turned up the lamp, and who should be at the door, United States Marshal Dyer and Deputy Marshal Vandercook, who made the arrest, subpoenaed my wife, Sarah and we went down to my wife Mary, who was soon in tears. She also was subpoenaed." George pleaded guilty to charges of cohabitation and was sentenced to six months in the Utah Penitentiary and a fifty-dollar fine.[18]

Plural Families during the Raid

Couples continued to marry polygamously during the Raid despite the threat of fines and imprisonment, but it quickened an already decreasing trend of plural marriages.[19] During this period, it was necessary to keep plural unions secret, even from close family and friends. In December 1883, Annie Clark married Joseph Marion Tanner as his second wife. After the marriage ceremony, Annie returned home alone to her family and later recounted: "As I sat down to a glass of bread and milk the thought came to me. 'Well, this is my wedding supper.' In those few minutes I recalled the elaborate marriage festivals which had taken place in our own family, of the banquets I had helped to prepare and the many lovely brides among my friends. . . . I was conscious of the obscurity of my own first evening after marriage. 'What a contrast,' I said to myself. 'No one will ever congratulate *me*.' Yet I was sure I had taken the right step."[20]

During these tenuous years, plural families had to be vigilant and created strategies to protect themselves. Husbands and plural wives who refused to abandon one another had limited options: they could face legal prosecution, hide on the "underground," or go into exile.

Many families took their chances on the underground, which meant they went into hiding. Men were safest living solely with their first and legal wife; thus, the majority did so.

Women hid to avoid incriminating their husbands for unlawful cohabitation or to avoid testifying against them in court if they had received subpoenas. Some on the underground remained at home and briefly hid as needed; others moved frequently, staying with friends and relatives or taking refuge in obscure places. Still others permanently relocated to other cities, states, or even countries under assumed names.

Pregnant plural wives and their children were obvious evidence of cohabitation, and the most common reason a woman would go into hiding was because of pregnancy. A newlywed plural wife, such as Mary Elizabeth Woolley Chamberlain, could seamlessly resume her "single" life until she became obviously pregnant. When that occurred, Mary wrote, "it became necessary for me to quit work and seek seclusion." A plural wife might travel alone or take some or all of her children into hiding, posing as a widow or single mother. Mary wrote, "It was a great trial to me to be separated from my husband and all my loved ones, and to drop completely out of sight with nothing at all to do." Despite her troubles, she wrote, "I never have regretted [becoming a plural wife] for one moment, but have ever been proud and thankful to be the wife of such a noble man."[21]

Men were often tied to a location due to employment, Church responsibilities, or agricultural demands. For this reason, many men hid near or within their own homes, taking refuge in a secret room or nearby irrigation ditch when deputies were nearby. Some, however, found it necessary to take more extreme measures and hid on the underground or lived in exile. Others were called to serve missions. In addition to battling loneliness, stress, and anxiety, many polygamous families struggled financially due to constant travel, isolation, and instability. Husbands in hiding, serving missions, or in prison were limited in their ability to provide monetary support, making financial situations particularly difficult during the Raid.

Establishment of Settlements in Mexico and Canada, 1885–87

As an alternative to living on the underground, the Church purchased land in Mexico and Canada to establish communities, or colonies, where the Saints could openly practice polygamy without legal prosecution. Beginning in 1885, hundreds of polygamous families moved to Mexico and established nine settlements. Among them were Colonia Juárez and Colonia Dublán, towns that still prosper today. Although polygamy was illegal in Mexico, Mexican authorities agreed not to enforce the law in order to encourage immigration. Latter-day Saints began settling in Alberta, Canada, in 1887. Polygamy was also illegal in Canada, so typically just one plural wife would live there. Latter-day Saint communities in Canada, such as Cardston, still thrive. These satellite communities gave plural families a freedom not experienced in the United States.

The Steady Decline

The number of plural marriages continued to decline. In the community of Manti, only 25.1 percent of the population were in polygamous families by 1880, a decline of almost half since 1860.[22] In the end, however, it was not merely the lack of participation, the railroad, or even legislation that brought the demise of polygamy—it was "vision and revelation."[23]

Manifesto, 1890

Antipolygamy legislation became so oppressive to the Church, its polygamous membership, and Utah's political quest for statehood that matters soon came to a head. Legal representatives of the Church in Washington, DC, had relentlessly challenged the lawfulness of the Edmunds-Tucker Act. The final blow came on May 19, 1890, when the US Supreme Court upheld the Edmunds-Tucker Act as constitutional.[24] Now the Church had exhausted all avenues of recourse. In a journal entry dated September 25, 1890, President Wilford Woodruff wrote, "I have arived at a point in the History of my life as the President of the Church of Jesus Christ of Latter

Day Saints where I am under the necessity of acting for the Temporal Salvation of the Church. . . . And after praying to the Lord & feeling inspired by his spirit I have issued the following Proclamation."[25]

In President Woodruff's publicly issued proclamation, commonly known as "the Manifesto," he advised Latter-day Saints to "refrain from contracting any marriages forbidden by the law of the land" (D&C, OD 1). The Manifesto was first sent as a press release and published in newspapers on September 25, 1890. For many Church members, the directive "came like a Thunderbolt out of the clear sky, for it had always been presumed that what ever would happen we would never surrender a principle."[26] Moreover, the Manifesto did not clarify the status of existing plural marriages: the Saints were unsure if President Woodruff was instructing current plural families to sever ties or if this directive applied only to future plural marriages.

At the Church's general conference less than two weeks later, the Manifesto was read over the pulpit and the congregation voted it "authoritative and binding." Individuals in the vast gathering noted that "many of the saints seemed stunned and confused and hardly knew how to vote . . . [and thus] refrained from voting."[27] One diarist observed that "many of the sisters weeped silently," and another noted that there was "great sadness and sorrow in the hearts of many" in attendance.[28]

Annie Gardner, plural wife of John Gardner, was present and recounted: "I was there in the Tabernacle the day of the Manifesto and I tell you it was an awful feeling. There Pres. Woodruff read the Manifesto that made me no longer a wife and might make me homeless. I sat there by my mother and she looked at me and said, 'How can you stand this?' But I voted for it because it [was] the only thing to do. I raised my hand and voted a thing that would make me an unlawful wife."[29]

Word of the Manifesto spread. Some Saints readily accepted the announcement. Annie Clark Tanner, who was both a plural wife and a descendant of polygamists, was on the underground in Franklin, Idaho, when she learned of the Manifesto. "I was easily convinced that it was from the Lord," she recorded. "I can remember so well the relief that I felt when I first realized that the Church had decided to abandon its position."[30]

For other members, the Manifesto was a bitter trial. Lorena Washburn Larsen, plural wife of Bent Larsen, was traveling with her husband to yet another home for their family when she heard the news. She recalled,

> My feelings were past description. . . . It seemed impossible that the Lord would go back on a principal which had caused so much sacrifice, heartache, and trial. . . .
>
> My anguish was inexpressible, and a dense darkness took hold of my mind. I thot that if the Lord and the church athorities had gone back on that principle, there was nothing to any part of the gospel. . . . I sank down on our bedding and wished in my anguish that the earth would open and take me and my children in. The darkness seemed impenetrable.
>
> All at once I heard a voice and felt a most powerful presence. The voice said, "Why this is no more unreasonable than the requirement the Lord made of Abraham when he commanded him to offer up his son Isaac, and when the Lord sees that you are willing to obey in all things the trial shall be removed."
>
> There was a light whose brightness cannot be described which filled my soul, and I was so filled with joy, peace, and happiness that I felt that no matter whatever should come to me in all my future life, I could never feel sad again.[31]

Although plural marriage was not rejected as a principle of the Latter-day Saint faith, the 1890 Manifesto stemmed the tide of most new plural marriages in the United States. It did not, however, immediately end the practice completely. Just as acceptance of polygamy took time to begin, discontinuing it was also a gradual process.

CHAPTER 6

POST-MANIFESTO AND BEYOND

"How peculiar the change after more than 40 years."

—Emmeline B. Wells, 1890[1]

Ambiguity filled the years following the 1890 Manifesto as members of The Church of Jesus Christ of Latter-day Saints transitioned from practicing plural marriage despite its illegality to navigating plurality within the "law of the land" (D&C, OD 1). Whether members were monogamous or polygamous, the principle and practice of plural marriage was so firmly ingrained in the Latter-day Saint mind that the change proved difficult. What did the future hold for those committed to this doctrine?

Some Church members lamented not marrying polygamously when they had the opportunity. A week after the Manifesto was sustained in general conference, monogamist John B. Fairbanks, who was serving as a missionary in Paris, exchanged a series of letters with his wife, Lillie. He expressed "a kind of regret that I had not entered into that principle before the privilege was denighed."[2] His wife, echoing his sentiments, wrote, "I don't feel well about it [the Manifesto], there is no chance for us."[3] John responded to Lillie's concern, "If the Lord does not require it of us Lillie then we are justified and will get the same reward as if we had entered that principle."[4]

During this transitional period, a small number of plural marriages continued to occur with special permission from specific Church authorities. The majority of these post-Manifesto marriage ceremonies took place in Canada and Mexico, although some were performed in the United States and even at sea.[5] Most Latter-day Saints, however, accepted the Manifesto at face value and began assimilating into monogamous marriage culture.

What Did Families Do?

With the law prohibiting plural marriages and Church leaders discouraging them, it was up to individual polygamous families to determine their own course. Some men abandoned their plural wives and children, an action that was roundly condemned. Other couples amicably separated. However, the majority of Latter-day Saints, including General Authorities, continued relations with their plural families, interpreting the Manifesto to mean that only no new plural marriages could occur.[6]

Amnesty for Polygamists, 1893

Seeking legal reprieve for Church members, in 1891 the First Presidency petitioned the president of the United States for amnesty for polygamists so that they would no longer be prosecuted for past marriages. Church leaders requested that those who had entered into the practice prior to November 1, 1890, be exempt from the penalties of law. On January 4, 1893, US President Benjamin Harrison granted amnesty on condition that no "further offence" occur.[7]

Although no "further offence" technically meant no further cohabitation, many plural husbands continued to live in multiple residences and father children well past 1890. Those who cohabited would still sporadically be arrested, but attitudes had eased, and cases were routinely dismissed.[8] In general, a husband moved with greater freedom between his families, wives took their husband's surname, and a great burden was lifted for many people. The only group that continued to live on the underground were post-Manifesto wives, since they were evidence that the illegal practice continued.

Utah Statehood, 1896

Utah became a territory of the United States in 1850, and though territories had a degree of independence, residents were eager to attain the full autonomy of statehood. After numerous application attempts for statehood failed, in part because of the Saints' practice of polygamy, Utah's proposed state constitution was finally accepted in 1895 by the federal government.[9] With Utah's constitution assuring that polygamy would be "forever prohibited," statehood was granted on January 4, 1896.[10]

Reed Smoot Hearings and the Second Manifesto, 1904–7

Apostle Reed Smoot was elected to the US Senate by the Utah legislature in 1903. Senator Smoot was a monogamist, but his high ecclesiastical position as a member of the Quorum of the Twelve ignited a nationwide protest. People were deeply suspicious of The Church of Jesus Christ of Latter-day Saints and its religious monopoly in Utah and still associated the Church with polygamy. Smoot, as a prominent leader of this group, was similarly viewed with suspicion—could he properly balance the separation of church and state? Congressional court hearings to determine if there could be a religious disqualification for Senate membership began in 1904 and continued through 1907. President Joseph F. Smith and others were called to the witness stand, and the case reopened questions about polygamy and revealed the threads of its continued practice. Because many polygamists, including President Smith, still cohabited with their plural wives and small numbers of post-Manifesto marriages had occurred, it called into question the Church's reported abandonment of the practice.[11]

To confirm to both members and nonmembers the Church's unequivocal stance to discontinue polygamy, President Joseph F. Smith issued a Second Manifesto in general conference in April 1904 and banned new plural marriages globally. In his official statement, he declared, "all such marriages are prohibited, and if any officer or member of the Church shall assume to solemnize or enter into any such marriage he will be deemed in transgression against the Church . . . and excommunicated therefrom."[12]

This prohibition did not apply to existing plural families, but after the Second Manifesto, again, some plural families chose to separate while others continued to quietly cohabit for the rest of their lives. For Latter-day Saints who continued to perform new polygamous marriages, the Second Manifesto marked a clear point of departure from the Church. They were excommunicated, and schismatic groups continue the practice of polygamy today.

Two Apostles Removed from the Quorum, 1905

In the wake of the Smoot hearings, Apostles Matthias F. Cowley and John W. Taylor, son of President John Taylor, came under scrutiny for officiating plural marriage ceremonies and for personally marrying plural wives after the 1890 Manifesto (as did other members of the Twelve before 1904).[13] Their actions again cast public doubt on the sincerity of Church leaders' commitment to abolish polygamy. Under pressure, Elders Taylor and Cowley resigned from the Quorum of the Twelve on October 28, 1905. Neither man returned to the Quorum of the Twelve, and in 1911 John W. Taylor was excommunicated. Cowley returned to full fellowship with the Saints.

The Dying Out of Polygamy

Some historians mark the real end of the polygamous era with the death of Joseph F. Smith in 1918, the last of the "pioneer prophets."[14] Polygamy soon faded into the background. Although some of the oldest Latter-day Saint polygamists lived into the 1960s, polygamy became a relic of the past in The Church of Jesus Christ of Latter-day Saints.

Gordon B. Hinckley, President of the Church from 1995 to 2008, reinforced the Church's modern stance on plural marriage, stating, "More than a century ago God clearly revealed unto his prophet Wilford Woodruff that the practice of plural marriage should be discontinued, which means that it is now against the law of God. Even in countries where civil or religious law allows polygamy, the Church teaches that marriage must be monogamous and does not accept into its membership those practicing plural marriage."[15] Any Latter-day Saints found to be practicing plural marriage today are excommunicated.

SECTION II

POLYGAMY—HOW AND WHY

CHAPTER 7

HOW DID POLYGAMY WORK?

"We obeyed the best we knew how, and no doubt, made many crooked paths in our ignorance."
—Amasa Lyman, 1866

For members of The Church of Jesus Christ of Latter-day Saints who chose to live polygamously, making the system of plural marriage "work" required some ground rules and the ability to occasionally pivot. This chapter discusses the "nuts and bolts" of polygamy—how plural marriage functioned for many Latter-day Saints. Unlike societies in which polygamy was a long-standing tradition, the Saints were still ironing out difficulties of the system by 1890, when the end of the practice was announced. As Amasa Lyman stated, "We obeyed the best we knew how, and no doubt, made many crooked paths in our ignorance."[1]

Permission to Marry Plurally

Not everyone who desired to marry plurally could enter into a polygamous union. For men, there was a highly centralized process for pursuing a plural marriage: all plural marriages had to be approved by the President of the Church.[2] This precedent was set by Joseph Smith to regulate the practice and to—ideally—ensure that all polygamists were "honorable and worthy" members who would "observe the laws of the Gospel and live their religion."[3] In addition, before taking "the least step" toward pursuing another wife, a husband was to ask his first wife for permission and receive her consent.[4]

Plural husbands-to-be typically initiated the permissions process. To receive permission from the President of the Church, some wrote directly to him, while others sought a letter of recommendation from an ecclesiastical leader, often their bishop or stake president, that attested to the man's worthiness and good standing in the Church. Because it was impossible for Church Presidents to personally know the worthiness of every applicant, they trusted the judgment of local leaders.[5] For example, a letter dated February 1, 1857, and addressed to Brigham Young from Bishop Joseph Harker of West Jordan, Utah, reads: "Sir, Bro. Ira K. Hillman wishes to have permission to take another wife[.] i can recommend him to be a faithfull and energetick man in the kingdom of our God and punctule in paying tithing."[6] Interestingly, the recommend did not include any information about the prospective bride; her worthiness and good standing were apparently assumed. A note dated February 12, 1857, from Brigham Young's office is inscribed on the letter, stating, "Go ahead." Ten days later, Ira married his second wife, Emma Baker.

Not every request was met with approval, however. Brigham Young offered the following reply in 1860 to frontiersman Peter Shirts, who was husband to three wives and requested permission to marry another. President Young wrote, "Until you can tame your thoughts and actions so far as to be willing to live where a family can be safe and have a reasonable opportunity for social enjoyment and improvement, I am of the opinion that it will be altogether best for you to continue to lead the life of a hermit, for I know of no woman worth a groat who would be willing to agree with your wild unsocial ways for any length of time."[7]

After obtaining permission from his first wife and the Church President, a prospective husband was then to receive the permission of the woman's parents and then finally of the woman herself.[8] This was the ideal pattern, but the reality was not always so straightforward. While first wives often consented for their husbands to marry another wife, some did not.[9] For some couples, a wife's refusal would close the issue. But, in the revelation on plural marriage, a wife's consent was *requested* but was not *required* (see D&C 132:65). If a first wife refused permission, the Church might permit a man to marry a plural wife anyway, if the first wife had no "acceptable" reason for why he should not marry again.[10] Thus, if a husband was persistent, a first wife might have felt her hands were tied, perhaps echoing the sentiment of first wife Ruth May Fox, who said, "I gave my consent, but I was human and resented it."[11]

Courtship

Because religious faith was such a strong motivator for practicing polygamy, some women were more concerned about marrying men who were righteous priesthood holders than marrying men to whom they were romantically attracted. Similarly, some men did not want to marry polygamously and may not have been romantically attracted to prospective plural wives, but they chose to marry again because they felt it their religious duty to do so.

Courtship in the polygamous system was unconventional. A relationship could be initiated by the prospective husband, the prospective bride, or even a wife. Many women who became plural wives experienced little to no courtship, which appealed to Victorian sensitivities about the appropriate behavior of married men. Mary E. Croshaw Farrell, fourth wife of George L. Farrell, said, "Married men didn't do any courting of their plural wives. Why, we would have thought it dishonorable for a mature married man to go sparking around like a young man. They just came and asked us, and if we wanted them, we agreed."[12]

Plural couples, of course, had varied experiences. In a discreet and lengthy courtship, Jesse W. Fox Jr. initiated a correspondence with Rosemary Johnson that spanned two years before she agreed to marry him in 1888. Rachel Woolley Simmons's husband, Joseph, was "infactuated" with Emma Bloxom and was determined to make her his second wife. Rachel recalled, "It wouldn't have been so hard if [Joseph] had not courted her so strong. . . . Joe used to go every other night to see her, and I thought that was too much when he had a family at home, but it made no difference what I thought."[13] Joseph and Emma married in August 1855.

Place of Marriage

After the Saints arrived in the Salt Lake Valley in 1847, marriage sealings were conducted in homes, on the second floor of Brigham Young's office, or on the top floor of Salt Lake City's Council House. In 1855, a temporary temple called the Endowment House was built on Temple Square. Most plural sealings over the next thirty years occurred there; some also took place in the St. George Temple after its dedication in 1877. The later Logan and Salt Lake Temples were dedicated in 1888 and 1893, respectively, and few live plural sealings were performed by that time.

Plural Marriage Sealing Ceremony

Apostle Orson Pratt wrote a monthly periodical called *The Seer*, in which he published the entire plural marriage sealing ceremony in 1853.[14] The plural marriage sealing ceremony was centered on principles of agency and consent and usually involved three participants: the first wife, her husband, and the bride. At the beginning of the ceremony, the first wife was asked, "Are you willing to give this woman to your husband to be his lawful and wedded wife for time and for all eternity?" Manifesting her consent, the first wife placed the bride's right hand into the right hand of her husband. The husband was then asked if he would receive the bride as his "lawful and wedded wife" by his "own free will and choice." After he agreed, the officiator asked the bride if she gave herself to the groom by her "own free will and choice." She then agreed.[15] The officiator then pronounced the new couple "husband and wife for time and for all eternity" and promised additional eternal blessings.[16]

Number of Latter-day Saints Who Practiced Polygamy

The total number of Latter-day Saints who practiced plural marriage is unknown. Existing records are incomplete and complicated, and not all are publicly available. However, a few focused local studies do give general statistics.

Historian Kathryn Daynes has shown that the community of Manti, Utah, is a reliable representation of general polygamy trends in Utah. Plural marriage reached its peak in Utah between 1855 and 1857, during a period of intense preaching on the subject. Thus, the 1860 US Federal Census records the highest percentage of polygamists: 43.1 percent of Manti residents belonged to a plural family as a husband, wife, or child. That number steadily declined over the next three decades to 36 percent in 1870, 25.1 percent in 1880, and only 7.1 percent in 1900.[17] If Manti's statistics reflect Utah's population as a whole, then tens of thousands of men, women, and children belonged to polygamous households at some point in their lives.[18]

Studies also illustrate that statistics varied between communities and were affected by socioeconomic factors. In Orderville, where Latter-day Saints lived the united order,[19] as many as 66.6 percent of Latter-day Saint families were polygamous in 1880. Thirty miles away in tiny Rockville, only 10.2 percent practiced polygamy, while in nearby Springdale, 36 percent were in plural families.[20]

The change in numbers from one city block to the next could be dramatic. Three adjacent congregations, called wards, in Salt Lake City had significantly different numbers of plural families in 1860. In the Fourteenth Ward, 46 percent of families were polygamous, while in the neighboring Seventeenth Ward, 38 percent were polygamous. Sharing a border with the Fourteenth Ward was the Seventh Ward, in which only 18 percent were polygamous families. Within the boundaries of the Fourteenth and Seventeenth Wards lived more prosperous families, including many General Authorities, who were more likely to have plural wives.[21]

Number of Wives

In general, the most visible leaders of the Church practiced plural marriage. This was true for men as well as women; from the President of the Church to the President of the Relief Society, polygamists set the standard of obedience for Church members. The majority of female general leaders in the Relief Society, Young Women, and Primary organizations belonged to polygamous families, and virtually every General Authority had multiple wives, as did most stake presidents and bishops.[22]

Brigham Young, the iconic polygamist, had fifty-five wives, and Heber C. Kimball had forty-three. Other polygamous husbands had far fewer wives. According to one demographic study, most polygamous men (66.3 percent) married only one plural wife. Thereafter, 21.2 percent married three women, 6.7 percent married four, and 5.8 percent married five or more women.[23]

Ages of Spouses

A common misconception is that many polygamists were elderly men who married young women. Plural wives were often younger than their husbands, as was broadly the case in monogamous marriages, but the age differences were generally not as radical as stereotypes depicted. A man usually married his first wife in his early twenties while his wife was in her late teens. If he married a second wife, 75 percent would have done so by age thirty-five. If he married a third, he likely would have done so by age forty. The majority of men who married a fourth wife did so between the ages of thirty-six and forty-five.[24] The average age at which a man stopped marrying was forty.[25] The ages of women at their time of marriage did not mirror the age variabilities of men, and the overwhelming majority of plural wives married for the first time before age twenty-five.[26]

There were exceptions, of course. At age thirty-eight, "spinster" Martha Spence married Joseph Heywood as a plural wife, a man several years her junior. On their first anniversary, she wrote rapturously of their precious newborn babe and the joy of "having a husband to care and watch over me that I feel to reverence, love and esteem and connected with a family that I am proud to be a member of, and realize that I am much happier now than I was a year ago."[27]

For marriages between young women and much older men, there was sometimes an element of coercion or obligation. Karen Kirstine Poulsen, an emigrant from Denmark, was fourteen years old when Herman J. Christensen, age thirty-seven, asked that she become his third wife. Herman was a prosperous Church and civic leader in their community, and Karen Kirstine's parents told her to marry him because he was "a wealthy man and could take care of her." She reluctantly accepted his proposal and cried the morning of their wedding on July 23, 1858.[28]

Some women deliberately chose an older husband. One extreme example is second wife Mary Jane McCleve, who recounted: "I was married Nov. 12 [1856] to Dr. Priddy Meeks who was 61 and I 16. It was love at first sight, even though he had three grown girls older than myself. . . . Ten children blessed our union."[29] Priddy wrote in his journal: "People may say what they want about mismated in age in marriage, but the Lord knows best about these matters. And if ever there was a match consummated by the providences of God this was one."[30]

"Polygamy in Low Life"

The Saints' relative isolation in the Mountain West left polygamy much to the outsider's imagination. Newspapers and books often presented wildly sensationalized views of polygamy, and Latter-day Saints, particularly women, felt profoundly misrepresented. "We are accustomed to hearing wonderful tales of the horrors of Mormon women," wrote plural wife Kirstine Christensen Baird. "We only laugh in our own minds at the stories told about our hardships, and grim looks and feelings."[31] But a photograph, in which viewers see real people, may not have been as easily dismissed. The image below, titled "Polygamy in Low Life," was said to depict a man and his five wives. Prints sold widely. Here is its story:

In the fall of 1870, Utah photographer Charles Roscoe Savage and Union Pacific Railroad photographer Andrew J. Russell stopped by the home of Savage's friends, monogamists Samuel and Mary Bunting Ashton, in Kaysville, Utah. Mary's three sisters and mother, Ann Slater Bunting, were also visiting. Noting that both photographers had their cameras, Ann Bunting asked that a picture be taken of her family. "Of course I assented," wrote C. R. Savage, and he arranged the family members present and took their picture. Afterward, Russell photographed them also, as he "desired to have a picture of a 'Mormon' country home." "I took no further notice of the matter," related C. R. Savage, "never [having] a doubt or suspicion of [Russell's] picture being used to the damage of the 'Mormon' community." Savage was shocked to learn that the photograph was later exhibited in New York

Courtesy Church History Library

City as "Polygamy in Low Life" by Russell, "who knew well that he was publishing a lie," wrote Savage. The Saints felt the photograph only fed the popular negative perception of polygamy and further misrepresented the reality of the practice in their communities.[32]

Living Arrangements

Housing arrangements among plural families did not follow a standard pattern and were affected by factors such as finances, locale, time period, the number and ages of children, and personal desires. In the early days of frontier settlement, many plural families lived together under one roof. In fact, Latter-day Saints developed an architectural innovation to accommodate this: one large home divided into independent sections for each wife. Brigham Young's famous Lion House was home to at least twelve wives and dozens of children, with each wife having her own bedroom and sitting area to receive visitors.[33]

For other plural families, living together was only temporary until separate residences could be built. Still other plural families lived separately from the start, either as near neighbors or placed strategically to help cultivate new settlements hundreds of miles apart. As the federal government passed laws criminalizing polygamy and began raiding homes in the 1880s, most large polygamous homesteads vanished, forcing families to live apart or go into hiding.

Visiting Patterns

For families who lived in separate residences, husbands' visiting patterns varied based on their proximity and individual circumstances. During peaceful periods, men might visit their wives on a nightly or weekly rotation. Other men lived primarily with their first and legal wife, particularly during the Raid, and visited plural families on the weekends, at harvest time, or during general conference twice a year. Some men's visits had no set pattern.

Wives responded differently to a husband's visits. Some women lived in anticipation of them; others did not. Martha Hughes Cannon, a plural wife and the first female state senator in the United States, quipped, "A plural wife is not half as much a slave as a single wife. If her husband has four wives she has three weeks of freedom every single month."[34]

Distribution of Wealth and Goods

One Latter-day Saint described plural marriages as "far too costly for the mass of our men," considering they would need to support multiple properties, households, and numerous children.[35] Leaders of the Church were wealthier on average than other Latter-day Saint men and were more likely to practice polygamy.[36] As wealthy men married plurally, it raised the standard of living for some women and helped to equalize the distribution of wealth per capita.[37] Although the most visible demographic of polygamists were wealthy ecclesiastical leaders, plural wives married men in all economic classes.

Individual families determined how to distribute wealth and goods among members. In some cases, families distributed goods equally, while others distributed money and goods according to the size of each family (that is, a wife with many children would get more than a wife with fewer children). In other families, unfortunately, one wife might be favored over another, and one would live comfortably while another struggled. In many polygamous families, women found ways to provide for themselves, not able to rely solely on a husband's income.

Clarissa Wilhelm Williams, a widow with four children, continued her employment as a laundress once she became a plural wife in 1851. She soon became frustrated with how her husband distributed income among his families and wrote, "I could not stand it any longer so I concluded to run my own shebang." She bought property "and got Lumber to build me A small house."[38] Clarissa remained married but claimed financial independence for herself and children.

Women as Heads of Household

Elizabeth Kane, the wife of respected politician Thomas L. Kane and not a Latter-day Saint, noted that "so many [Latter-day Saint women] seem to have the entire management, not only of their families, but of their households and even outside business affairs, as if they were widows."[39] This was true; because of polygamy and men's missionary service, more women were heads of households in Utah than elsewhere in the US. Latter-day Saints argued that cooperative effort between wives benefited a family's economy. They also pointed to the fact that married women in Utah could hold property in their own names, an anomaly in the United States, providing greater independence. When polygamous men were accused of being unable to care for their large families, forcing women to care for themselves, Latter-day Saint women might have responded that supporting their families gave them opportunities for work and education, expanding their sphere in society to include both a family and a satisfying profession.[40] Martha Hughes Cannon stated, "You give me a woman who thinks about something besides cook stoves and wash tubs and baby flannels and I'll show you nine times out of ten a successful mother."[41]

Women supported themselves in traditional female careers as midwives, teachers, and seamstresses but also explored innovative avenues for income. While the husband of first wife Ellen Larson Smith struggled to sustain his second family in Utah, Ellen acquired a camera and soon had a thriving photography business in Snowflake, Arizona. Ellen earned additional income through beekeeping, housecleaning, and operating a notions shop.[42] Some plural wives also helped support their sister wives. Patty Sessions, a noted midwife, not only provided for herself but also helped provide for her sister wife, Harriet, who had young children.[43]

Sadly, other plural wives were left destitute, without means to meet their or their children's needs. Josephine Streeper Chase confided in her diary after the visit of her husband, whom she called Pa, "I think pa is very hard on me to go and leave me with out one cent and tell me to do the best i can[.] . . . I am broken hearted, But i try to trust in the Lord."[44] Financial abandonment was a common reason for divorce among polygamists.

Divorce

In nineteenth-century America, most states had laws that made it difficult for couples to divorce. Utah was an exception to this rule, essentially allowing no-fault divorces. Just as marriage was different in Utah, so too was divorce. Two marriage systems existed in Utah until the 1880s: a legal system and an ecclesiastical system. The legal system allowed a man to have only one legal wife—his first wife. Under the ecclesiastical system, men married plural wives through Church ordinances. These marriages were considered legitimate and "lawful" only by Church members and were not considered legal marriages by anyone else. Consequently, there were also two types of divorces: legal and ecclesiastical. Civil courts typically handled the dissolution of first marriages (those acknowledged by law), and ecclesiastical courts dissolved polygamous marriages.

In divorce cases in Utah, there were frequently "no lawyers, no grounds stated, no waiting period for the divorce to become final, and [there was] evidence of cooperation to obtain the divorce."[45] First wife Jane Snyder Richards affirmed, "If a marriage is unhappy, the parties can go to any of the council, present their difficulties and are readily granted a divorce."[46] Although Brigham Young and other General Authorities preached against divorce, President Young was liberal in granting women divorces.[47] His advice to women was to "stay with her husband as long as she could bear with him, but if life became too burdensome, then leave and get a divorce."[48]

The comparative ease of obtaining a divorce does not imply that divorce was a flippant decision; Church and social sanctions were too strong.[49] But divorce in Utah was quite common during this period, and it did not carry the same social stigma among Latter-day Saints that it did elsewhere. People in prominent Church positions sometimes had multiple divorces. Indeed, Presidents Brigham Young, Wilford Woodruff, and

Joseph F. Smith all experienced divorce.[50] A divorced woman could and would often remarry, and she sometimes remarried again as a plural wife.[51]

Hannah Thompson married John R. Winder as his second wife in 1855. In her autobiography, Hannah recorded that in 1864, she

> wrote a kind letter to Brother Winder, and planely informed him that it had been nearly 4 years since he had deprived me of a Husbands attention and affection, and that nothing short of him keeping the covenants that he had made with me in the House of the Lord would do, and that I would take steps to have a separation. My letter was not answered, neither would he come to talk with me. I then went to President Young's Office and signed my divorce with his consent and left it there for Brother Winder's signature. He signed it and sent it to me. He also sent a pair of shoes for [our daughter,] Anna.[52]

Hannah married Ariah C. Brower as his fifth wife in 1865.

Number of Divorces

Determining the number of divorces among plural families is inconclusive due to incomplete records, but it appears that the Church granted about 1,900 divorces between 1847 and 1886.[53] The bulk of these divorces were sanctioned by Brigham Young, who granted 1,645 divorces during his presidency (1847–77).[54] In Utah in 1870, there was one divorce for every 185 legally married couples, giving Utah the second highest divorce rate in the United States, with only Wyoming ranking higher. If the number of ecclesiastical divorces were added to that figure, however, Utah likely had the highest divorce rate in the nation.[55]

A local case study in Manti, Utah, again provides a more detailed view of trends over time. Of 465 total plural marriages, 83 of those marriages ended in divorce, equating to a divorce rate of 17.8 percent. However, examining the number of divorced plural wives, first wives, and husbands separately reveals more about the divorce dynamic. One-fourth (24.6 percent) of all plural wives divorced their husbands. Far fewer first wives divorced their husbands (only 8 percent). Of 151 polygamous men in Manti, just over one-third (35.1 percent) were divorced at least once.[56]

Separation without Divorce

These numbers, however, do not reflect polygamous couples who separated without securing a formal divorce. Annie Clark Tanner recorded the visit of her husband, Marion, to her home in Farmington in 1912. He was an infrequent visitor, and when he arrived at their home, he informed her "that he would not come to Farmington to see us anymore," Annie wrote. "The statement was a great shock to me," she said, but "I thought in those few moments before he departed: 'I'll be equal to whatever must come.'"[57] Thus ended their thirty-year marriage.

Conclusion

There were high moral and religious expectations for Latter-day Saint polygamists, and they were committed to the practice of plural marriage by covenant. Although no standardized patterns governed how to live polygamously, the Saints were expected to care for their families. Not all lived up to these expectations; as Mary Jane Mount Tanner acknowledged in 1880, polygamy was "capable of being abused as marriage itself frequently is."[58] In situations where a plural union did not work, couples could easily divorce. Usually, however, the Saints who entered plural marriage sought, like Amasa Lyman, to make "crooked paths" straight and adapt to the plural marriage system, making it work for them and other imperfect human beings as they moved together toward a religious ideal.

CHAPTER 8

WHY PRACTICE POLYGAMY?

"Fit for an inheritance in
the Celestial Kingdom of God."
—*Joseph Smith, according to John Taylor, 1883*

Without question, the majority of Latter-day Saints who entered plural marriage did so because they believed God commanded it. They believed Joseph Smith was a prophet of God, and they had faith in the revelations he received. They believed the words of Church leaders and fellow Saints who preached polygamy as a divine principle. Though the reasons individual Saints chose to marry polygamously were usually grounded in theology and religious faith, their motivations at times also blended with temporal concerns, social pressure, and even romantic love. This chapter explores reasons why—both theological and otherwise—nineteenth-century Latter-day Saints chose to practice plural marriage, from their perspectives.

Scriptural and Theological Explanations

Joseph Smith left only one document addressing eternal and plural marriage, and it is canonized today as Doctrine and Covenants 132. That revelation, along with other scripture, outlines theological reasons why God sometimes allows plural marriage. These theological reasons were cited by Latter-day Saints in the nineteenth century to justify and defend the practice.

Multiply and Replenish the Earth

In the revelation on plural marriage, one reason given for plurality was to "multiply and replenish the earth" (D&C 132:63). In the Bible, Abraham was promised to have progeny as limitless as the sands of the seashore (Gen. 22:17). Latter-day Saints saw themselves as members of the restored house of Israel, called to help fulfill this Abrahamic covenant and, in so doing, becoming recipients of the same blessings (D&C 132:29–33). The Saints were not simply to produce children, however. God intended that they "raise up seed *unto me*," implying that, through plural marriage, a righteous man with multiple wives could father more children and thus raise a large and faithful posterity unto the Lord (Jacob 2:30; italics added).

Significantly, however, the Book of Mormon establishes monogamy as God's preferred order of marriage except if the Lord commanded polygamy to be instituted (Jacob 2:24, 27, 30). These scriptures specify that monogamy is the rule, but polygamy could, for a time, be the exception.

Restoration of All Things

In the nineteenth century, many Christians eagerly searched the scriptures for prophecies confirming that Jesus Christ's Second Coming was near. Early converts were excited by the Church's assertion that the "dispensation of the fulness of times" had commenced and would bring a final "restitution of all things," including a restoration of the laws, authority, ordinances, and blessings of previous dispensations (D&C 128:18; 132:40; Acts 3:21; Eph. 1:10).[1] Among those laws was plural marriage, practiced by the ancient patriarchs of the Old Testament, and many Saints accepted polygamy as being a component of the restoration that would precede the Second Coming.

As a young woman in England, Sarah Barnes joined the Church in 1842, believing that she had embraced "the same Gospel that the ancients had." After learning that the Latter-day Saints practiced polygamy, she wrote, "I could plainly see that if plural marriage was a principle of the Gospel then, it must of necessity be so now."[2] Sarah's conviction of the necessity of a restoration of all things, including the reintroduction of plural marriage, was reinforced by her study of the Bible and served as the foundation of her acceptance of polygamy, and she later became a plural wife.

Similarly, in restoring the Old Testament practice of polygamy in the latter days, the Saints believed they were fulfilling biblical prophecy. As a twelve-year-old girl working in a dress shop in the eastern United States in 1866, Latter-day Saint Ruth May Fox recalled that she had "a real opportunity to defend my religion" as her peers challenged her beliefs. She said, "Always polygamy would come up for discussion, but I was ready with my quotation from Isaiah: 'And in that day seven women shall take hold of one man, etc.'"[3] Like Ruth, many Saints read Isaiah's prophecy that in the last days "seven women shall take hold of one man, saying, We will eat our own bread, and wear our own apparel: only let us be called by thy name, to take away our reproach" (Isa. 4:1). Some believed that plural marriage fulfilled this prophecy. This scripture was often quoted by defenders of the practice, and it influenced men and women to marry polygamously because, in their view, they were living in the last days.

Abrahamic Sacrifice and the Trial of God's People

Since the restored Church had direct roots in the Old Testament and Latter-day Saints viewed themselves as modern Israel (God's people), they anticipated trials individually and collectively. Because Joseph Smith's revelation on plural marriage mentioned Abraham and the sacrifice of his son Isaac, many nineteenth-century Saints saw polygamy as an "Abrahamic test" intended to purify the Saints, akin to the Lord asking Abraham to sacrifice his beloved son Isaac (D&C 132:34–37, 50–51).[4] Enduring well an Abrahamic test—a trial that would "wrench your very heartstrings," said Joseph Smith—would help make one "fit for an inheritance in the Celestial Kingdom of God."[5] Although the parallel to

Abraham is imperfect, some Saints saw this as a viable explanation for why the Lord commanded the reinstitution of polygamy. They believed that by obeying the commandment of plural marriage, they would prove their devotion to God and, like Abraham, would be worthy to receive special blessings (see D&C 98:12–15).

More broadly, the Saints believed that because they were God's people, He required their trial and purification as a group. Artimesia Snow "freely gave [her] consent" for her husband, Apostle Erastus Snow, to marry a second wife in Nauvoo in 1844. "I have not been without my trials in the practice of this principle," she confessed. "The Lord has said, He would have a tried people, that they should come up through great tribulation, that they might be prepared to endure His presence and glory. If I had no trials, I should not expect to be numbered with the People of God, and therefore not be made a partaker of His blessings and glory."[6]

Polygamy created a sense of cohesion among the Latter-day Saints. God's people were always chastened in some way, the Saints believed, and polygamy was a shared trial that set them apart from other religious groups, reinforcing the idea that, through hardship, God was molding His chosen people. The practice also established an insular, protective sense of community. As the Saints gathered in the Mountain West, the sense of being a people set apart deepened. Church members not only created extensive family networks through plural marriage but also banded together to defend their religious beliefs from an outside world that persecuted, rejected, and mocked them.

Highest Heaven in the Celestial Kingdom

The promise of eternal blessings was perhaps the most compelling reason many Latter-day Saints married plurally. In 1832, Joseph Smith received a vision of heaven's three degrees of glory: the telestial, terrestrial, and celestial kingdoms (D&C 76). He learned that those who accepted the Atonement of Jesus Christ, were baptized by priesthood authority, received the Holy Ghost, and lived faithfully could gain salvation and enter the celestial kingdom, God's highest degree of glory (D&C 76:51–54, 94–95). It was further revealed in May 1843 that within the celestial kingdom there were three additional degrees of glory (D&C 131). The Saints believed that in order to be exalted into the highest degree of glory within the celestial kingdom, a man and woman must be married by the power of the priesthood and receive the sealing ordinance to bind their union eternally.[7] Thus, in Latter-day Saint theology, the sealing ordinance, or eternal marriage, opens the door to exaltation.

The understanding that eternal marriage could grant entrance into the highest heaven of the celestial kingdom certainly motivated Latter-day Saints to be sealed. But eternal marriages could be monogamous or polygamous. So, why did some take the difficult step to marry polygamously? In general, those in plural unions believed that they were obeying a higher law and thus qualified for greater celestial glory than monogamists, who could still be exalted in the celestial kingdom but with a lesser glory.[8]

Messages from Church leaders, however, were not always clear on this point. In 1866, Brigham Young stated, "The only men who become Gods, even the Sons of God, are those who enter into polygamy." Yet, in the same sermon he stated, "If you desire with all your hearts to obtain the blessings which Abraham obtained, you will be polygamists *at least in your faith*."[9] The two ideas appear to be contradictory: the first seems to indicate that plural marriage was essential to receive the highest eternal blessings, while the second implies that simple acceptance of the principle was all that was required, not its actual practice. Later, Brigham Young reiterated, "A Man may Embrace the Law of Celestial Marriage in his heart & not take the second wife & be justified before the Lord."[10]

In about 1867, monogamist John P. Hawley attended a meeting in which Brigham Young was asked "whether a man could obtain Celestial Glory with but one wife, and he answered he could, but not to the fullest extent of Glory," John later remembered. "This question and answer eased my mind some what on the Subject of multiplying wives as I had understood by B[righam] Youngs teachings before this that no man could obtain Selestial Glory unless he had come to the Law of multiplication."[11] With the reassurance that he could still attain celestial glory, John was among the majority of Latter-day Saints who remained monogamous.[12]

Still, confusion persisted. Misunderstanding allowed for folk doctrine to seep into local teachings. For example, there was an ambiguous teaching that the more women a man married, the greater his glory would be in the next life.[13] Some also believed that a man had to marry three wives (representing the Godhead) to reach the highest exaltation, to which Wilford Woodruff responded, that he "kn[e]w of no requirement" to that effect and clarified that marrying one additional wife fulfilled the law of plural marriage.[14]

As the Saints transitioned out of polygamy after the 1890 Manifesto, they attempted to disentangle doctrine from tradition and scripture from opinion-riddled sermons to create more unified teachings. In 1912, Charles W. Penrose, a polygamist and counselor in the First Presidency, responded to the question "Is plural or celestial marriage essential to a fulness of glory in the world to come?" with the following answer: "Celestial marriage is essential to a fulness of glory in the world to come, as explained in the revelation concerning it [D&C 132]; but it is not stated that plural marriage is thus essential." More recently, Elder Marcus B. Nash explained in 2015 that "the ordinance that seals couples for eternity includes identical covenants and blessings for monogamous marriages and for the authorized plural marriages performed in the past."[15] Thus the potential for exaltation for monogamous and polygamous couples is now understood to be equal.

It must be remembered that statements made by early Church leaders asserting the necessity of plural marriage were made when the commandment of plural marriage was in force and are not applicable to Church members today.

Other Explanations

Some Latter-day Saints chose to practice plural marriage for a variety of reasons. Though many of these reasons were deeply rooted in religious belief, not all had a scriptural foundation.

Testimony of the Gospel

Some Saints did not have a testimony of the principle of polygamy, but they did have a testimony of the truthfulness of the restored gospel. With that faith, they were able to accept plural marriage. Priscilla Merriman Evans, a Welsh convert, recalled when the "Principle of Plurality of Wives" was first preached in Wales in the 1850s, stating, "It caused quite a commotion in our branch. One of the girls came to me with tears in her eyes and said, 'Is it true that Brigham Young has ninety wives?[16] I can't stand that, Oh, I can't stand it.' I asked her how long it had been since I had heard her testify that she knew the Church was true, and I said if it was, then it is true now. I told her I did not see anything for her to cry about. After I talked to her awhile, she dried her eyes and completed her arrangements to get married and emigrate."[17]

Economic Support

Some viewed plural marriage as a way to care for the "fatherless and widows," including women who left troubled marriages (James 1:27). Sarah Peake Noon migrated to Nauvoo from England in 1841 with her husband, William, and their two young daughters. William was an abusive alcoholic, and Sarah separated from him when she was several months pregnant. In 1842, at the urging of Joseph Smith, Heber C. Kimball married Sarah as his first plural wife, and he cared for her and her children.[18]

In addition to providing greater economic stability for families, plural marriage also helped to "unite a diverse immigrant population," as converts from all over the world gathered to Latter-day Saint communities.[19] Clarissa Wilhelm Williams emigrated to the Salt Lake Valley in June 1851. Her husband died en route, leaving Clarissa a widow with four children. She struggled to acquire daily necessities and recorded in her autobiography: "I found it quite hard to bye wood and evrything I had so I thought to better my condition by marrying."[20] To improve her economic condition, she married David Lewis, captain of her emigrating company, as his second wife.

Ecclesiastical Position

Family and social pressure has played a role in marriage decisions for ages past, and those same pressures influenced some Latter-day Saints' plural marriage decisions, too. What was unique to the decision to enter into plural marriage, however, was its religious nature and the weight given to counsel from General Authorities. Latter-day Saint men who held Church leadership positions, including those in bishoprics or stake presidencies, were expected to model commitment to *all* of the principles of the restored gospel, including plural marriage. Thus, they were often counseled to marry plurally and generally felt it was their duty to comply.

Margaret McNeil Ballard shared her experience:

> My husband, being a Bishop, had been counseled by the authorities to set the example of obedience by entering into this law [of polygamy]. The compliance of this was a greater trial to my husband than it was to me. He would say, "Margaret, you are the only woman in the world I ever want." . . . While this was a trial for both of us we knew that the Lord expected us to be obedient in this law, as in all laws, as revealed in these the latter days. After many weeks of pondering and praying for guidance, I persuaded my husband to enter into this law and suggested to him my sister, Emily, three years younger than myself, as his second wife. . . .
>
> They decided to be married . . . in the Endowment House. Henry asked me to go with them on this trip. I made a protest as I was in a delicate condition [pregnant]. Henry was grieved and said to me, "Margaret, unless you

go with me and give your consent to this marriage and stand as a witness, I will not go." I went . . . and gave my consent and blessing to the union.[21]

Victorian Sexuality and Polygamy

People in the nineteenth century were simultaneously horrified and fascinated by the sexual possibilities of polygamy. During the Victorian era, there was a dramatic rise in prostitution, and it was considered one of the great social problems of the day. Those not of the Latter-day Saint faith considered polygamous marriages illegitimate and scorned plural wives as being adulterers, prostitutes, and concubines. Latter-day Saints perceived a great hypocrisy between accusations that they were sexually immoral while the sexual indiscretions of Victorian men, such as employing prostitutes, were at that time figuratively swept under the rug. Apostle Orson Pratt suggested that plural marriage was an antidote to fornication and adultery. In the August 1853 issue of *The Seer*, he took the stance of a social reformer, arguing that polygamy could eradicate prostitution because men would not be tempted to have extramarital relations and women would each have the opportunity to marry able providers (124–25). Elder Pratt's reasoning was not grounded in scripture or doctrine, but it became a popular defense of polygamy used by Latter-day Saints to publicly justify the practice.

Marriage and Motherhood

Nineteenth-century society was structured around the marriage relationship; historically, marriage allowed a woman to fulfill what were considered her highest social roles—those of a wife and mother. For a woman who desired to marry, plural marriage expanded her opportunities to find a husband. Church leaders, as well as Latter-day Saint women, claimed that polygamy elevated the status of women, ensuring they had the opportunity to become "honored wives and mothers with homes of their own and social position."[22]

Elizabeth Graham Macdonald felt passionately that each woman had a right to marry a devoted Latter-day Saint, experience motherhood, and receive the sealing ordinance if she desired. Thus, Elizabeth permitted her husband to marry four additional women, reasoning, "Why should I or any other woman in the Church with-hold this privilege from another because of the feelings of our weak nature."[23]

A Righteous Husband—A Surplus of Righteous Women

There was, and still is today, a general perception that righteous women outnumber righteous men and that more women will qualify for celestial glory than men. Some have suggested that this numerical inequality was an explanation for why plural marriage was instituted.[24] Although these ideas were pondered upon and even mentioned by Church leaders from the pulpit, they are speculative, and the conclusion that righteous women outnumber righteous men or that more women than men will qualify for the celestial kingdom is not scripturally supported.[25]

Because eternal marriage is essential to exaltation, Latter-day Saint women often chose to marry men—married or single—who were worthy to enter temples to be sealed. Thus, some couples prioritized righteousness, or worthiness, over romantic love. Elizabeth Kane recorded a conversation she had with a "lovely-looking woman" who "admitted that if she had married the young man whom she had once loved . . . and she had been henceforward his one darling wife that her *earthly* felicity might have been greater." But instead, she was baptized, migrated to Utah, and married polygamously to "receive the highest elevation in the next world" and was "perfectly satisfied with her condition as a plural wife, and thought her husband the best man on the whole earth."[26] Her choice to marry a righteous husband in polygamy was deliberate; it gave her the satisfaction of achieving her ultimate aim: an eternal reward through the sealing ordinance.

Additionally, there was a misconception that single women outnumbered single men in Utah, making plural marriage necessary. But such was not the case.[27] In fact, single men were consistently drawn to the territory due to mining and other trades. What is not known, however, is how many of these men Latter-day Saint women considered desirable marriage partners.

Infertility

Because one purpose of marriage was to multiply and replenish the earth, plural marriage was often seen as a solution if it seemed a wife could not have children. After nine childless years of marriage to Joseph Felt, Louie Bouton Felt sought out a second wife for her husband. Louie wrote, "[I] became thoroughly convinced of the truth of the principle of celestial marriage, and having no children of my own was very desirous my husband should take other wives that he might have a posterity to do him honor."[28] Louie then initiated a "proposal" to Elizabeth Mineer, who recalled that Louie "asked me if I would consider marrying her husband. I laughed at it at first, but later thought more about it."[29] Elizabeth and Joseph married in 1875 and had six children. In 1882, Joseph married a third wife, Elizabeth Liddell, and the couple had eight children.

Love

Some individuals married polygamously for love. George Kirkham recorded simply in his journal that he chose to marry his plural wife, Sara, because "she loved me and I did her."[30] Ida Hunt was in love with David K. Udall and became his second wife. On their wedding day, she gushed in her journal, "I was sealed for Time and all Eternity to David King Udall, the only man on Earth to whose care I could freely and gladly entrust my future. . . . May the deep unchangeable love which I feel for my husband today increase with every coming year helping me to prove worthy of the love and confidence which he imposes in me."[31]

Conclusion

Ca. 1890. Sisters Mary Russon (left) and Sara Russon (right) chose to marry George Kirkham, in 1872 and 1875, respectively.

Why practice plural marriage? Each Saint would likely answer that question differently based on his or her personal convictions and experiences. Many chose to practice plural marriage because of scriptural mandates to raise a righteous population and because of the promise of eternal blessings. The same testimony that inspired some members to join the Church also moved them to marry polygamously. Some chose plurality for temporal reasons, such as needing or lending economic support. Others elected to marry under direct counsel from Church leaders. For some Saints, plural marriage provided a worthy spouse and a longed-for opportunity for eternal marriage and parenthood. Those who married for love desired to be eternally united with a beloved. Others simply said, "I know not, save the Lord commanded me" (Moses 5:6). Ultimately, at the foundation of most Saints' choices to marry polygamously was a desire to follow what they believed was "the word and will of God."[32]

SECTION III

LISTENING TO LATTER-DAY SAINT VOICES

CHAPTER 9

PERSONAL JOURNEYS OF FAITH

"Nothing but a knowledge of God, and the revelations of God, and the truth of them, could have induced me to embrace such a principle as this."
—*John Taylor, 1883*

Although plural marriage was a path walked with others, it was a personal journey. The decision to marry polygamously was often approached prayerfully, and believers sought God's will through personal revelation and divine manifestations. Despite spiritual witnesses they may have received, individuals had human moments of conflicted emotions and personal pain as they evaluated entering polygamy and discovered how it shaped the trajectory of their lives.

Choosing Polygamy

When plural marriage was first introduced to individual Latter-day Saints, a pattern of horror, questioning, doubt, and earnest prayer often followed. "I had always entertained strict ideas of virtue, and I felt as a married man that this was . . . an appalling thing to do," said President John Taylor, reflecting the feelings he had after learning about polygamy in Nauvoo. "Nothing but a knowledge of God, and the revelations of God, and the truth of them, could have induced me to embrace such a principle as this."[1] This same conviction drove many Saints to enter plurality, but their decision did not come easily.

Personal Spiritual Witness

There was no set formula for receiving a spiritual witness to practice polygamy. Some experiences were dramatic: Jeanette Irvine McMurrin heard an audible voice telling her the name of the man she would marry as his second wife, and Mary Alice Springall Schoenfeld recognized her husband from a prophetic dream.[2] For others, answers came gradually.

There were Saints such as Cordelia Morley, whose initial rejection of polygamy slowly evolved to acceptance. In 1844, Joseph Smith asked Isaac and Lucy Gunn Morley for permission to marry their twenty-year-old daughter, Cordelia. Her parents introduced Cordelia to the new doctrine and extended Smith's marriage proposal. She refused, stating, "I [k]new nothing of such religion and could not except it neither did I." But her feelings changed over time, and she came to accept the doctrine. In 1846, Cordelia married Frederick Walter Cox in the Nauvoo Temple as his third wife and was sealed by proxy to the deceased Joseph Smith, honoring his initial request. After six years of marriage, outside pressures forced Cordelia to again confront her testimony of the principle. She wrote, "I began to worry & to wonder if I had in these years been so deceived. I longed for a testimony from my Father in Heaven to know for myself whether I was right or wrong. I was called a fallen woman—the finger of scorn was pointed at me. I felt that it was more than I could endure. In the humility of my soul I prayed that I might have a testimony from Him who knows the hearts of all." In a dream, "the spirit came to me and whispered in my ear these words, 'Don't ever change your condition or wish it otherwise,' for I was better off than thousands and thousands of others. This brought peace to my mind and I have felt satisfied ever since."[3]

In contrast, twenty-two-year-old Mary Christensen made her decision to become a plural wife in an instant. In 1886, Mary was being pressed for answers to several marriage proposals and, not knowing what to do, she knelt to pray. Mary recounted, "After having first closed the doors and pulled down the window blinds being ther[e] alone before the Lord that I asked Him that He would guide me and show me the man that I was to marry. And then it was at that very moment that A[ndrew] J. Hansen knocked on my door."[4]

Andrew, who had two wives, had come to Mary's home for the express purpose of proposing. Andrew remembered, "After talking to her pleasantly for a few minutes . . . I at once laid before her the object of my visit."[5] Mary replied, "I told him then and there that I did not feel that I had much to say about it. I had just a few moments before asked the Lord to show me the man I was to marry and that I had not gotten up from off my knees till he had knocked on the door. I told him that he would have been my last choice but that I was sure that he was the Lord's choice and I would accept of him."[6] Andrew concluded, "To future generations, who will have been brought up under Monogamic conditions the foregoing will no doubt seem absurd. . . . But I make no apologies, I owe none, Celestial, and Plural Marriage is a law of Heaven and at that time in force among Gods people on earth, sanctioned and approved by Him, and I knew it."[7]

Plans to Marry Polygamously

As early as the 1840s, some young women, knowing they wanted plural families, proactively selected a sister wife with whom they knew they could be happy even before marriage prospects came. For example, Sarah Barnes and her good friend Sarah Martin promised one another that they would marry the same man, and they did.[8] In the 1850s, sisters Sarah Maria and Amanda Mousley agreed "to share with each other, their lot in marriage" and were married to Angus Cannon on the same day.[9]

Two generations later, in the 1880s, young people were still making deliberate plans for plural marriage. During their courtship, Ellen Larson and Silas Smith vowed to marry one another and prayerfully "agreed that some day we would live the principle of polygamy."[10] Ellen and Silas married in 1886,

Courtesy Church History Library; edited by Keith N. Finlayson

Ellen Larson Smith (left) and Maria Bushman Smith (right), wives of Silas D. Smith, pictured with their children in Arizona, ca. 1902

and, abiding by their plan, Silas married his second wife, Maria Bushman, in 1888.

Whatever their experiences, for these early Saints, living the principle of plural marriage was a journey of faith. Many bore witness of spiritual experiences that strengthened their resolve. "I bear testimony that the revelation on Celestial marriage given through the prophet Joseph, is from God," declared Elizabeth Graham Macdonald. "In my experience I do know that the blessings and promises contained in that revelation are realized when lived for."[11]

Choosing Monogamy

Some Saints chose not to enter polygamous unions.[12] Sarah Sturtevant Leavitt, for example, was a faithful believer in the principle, but after a spiritual manifestation, she chose not to practice it. In her autobiography, she remembered her conversion to plural marriage in Nauvoo:

> I have thought for many years that the connections between man and wife were as sacred as the heavens and ought to be treated as such . . . but still I wanted a

> knowledge of the truth for myself. I asked my husband if he did not think we could get a revelation for ourselves on that subject. He said he did not know. After we went to bed I lay pondering it over in my mind. I said, "You know, Lord, that I have been a faithful and true wife to my husband, and you know how much I love him, and must I sacrifice him?" The answer was, "No."
>
> And then my mind was carried away from the earth and I had a view of the order of the celestial kingdom. I saw that was the order there and oh, how beautiful. I was filled with love and joy that was unspeakable. I awoke my husband and told him of the views I had and that the ordinance was from the Lord, but it would damn thousands. It was too sacred for fools to handle, for they would use it to gratify their lustful desires. How thankful we ought to be that we live in a day when we can know the will of God concerning our duty, and that the darkness that has so long covered the earth has been dispelled and the light of truth has burst upon the benighted world.[13]

Sarah's husband, Jeremiah, died in Iowa in 1846, and Sarah remained a widow for over thirty years.

Apostle Erastus Snow advised John Hawley to consider marrying a plural wife, and John became engaged to a woman in a neighboring community. "I could See that it would be a grate trial to my wife," he remembered, "and to tell you the truth it was also a trial to me but we was determand for exaltation." John made arrangements to travel with his betrothed to Salt Lake to be sealed, "but alas," he said, "my hart failed when I got ready for the trip." While driving his team to pick her up, he wrote, "I began to Seari[ou]sly reflect. . . . I resolved in my own hart to leave the girl . . . and we mutialy agreed to desolve the contract between us and when this was done I concluded to let E. Snows counsel lay idle and wate for a revelation from the lord."[14]

CHAPTER 10

RELATIONSHIPS AMONG HUSBAND AND WIVES

"[Marriage] unites man and woman together, and demands from each the highest and truest form of love."
—*Editorial,* Woman's Exponent, *1884*[1]

Polygamy was rooted in relationships, and the most basic relationship was between a husband and wife. Just as in monogamous marriages, plural spouses had varying experiences and challenges. So too, the feelings of polygamous husbands and wives often mirrored those of monogamists—they yearned for unity, companionship, and love and felt the pain of betrayal, frustration, and heartache—even as their situations were riddled with circumstances unique to plural unions. These circumstances included navigating complicated layers of family diplomacy, living independently of one's spouse, welcoming new wives into the family, and ultimately cultivating the love which, despite obstacles, bound many couples together.

Happiness for All: A Husband's Challenge

The reality of plural marriage was far from the male paradise depicted in steamy Victorian novels. Indeed, plural marriage marked the "beginning of all my sorrows," wrote Phineas Cook, "notwithstanding I was converted to the doctrine of plurality."[2] Men often found it challenging to be the head of multiple households and husband to multiple wives. As head of the family, a polygamous husband had the complicated responsibility to help meet the needs of each wife while fairly settling disputes and fostering harmonious relationships. In essence, his role was to try to keep everyone happy. Elizabeth Graham Macdonald praised her husband as being one "amongst a thousand" in his ability to keep his wives happy, knowing that domestic peace was sometimes elusive in polygamous households.[3] "Where is the man who has wives, and all of them think he is doing just right to them?" asked Brigham Young. "I do not know such a man; I know it is not your humble servant."[4]

"I find much annoyance and vexation of spirit as well as the schooling of the feelings in polygamy," wrote David Candland in 1859. "My wives Anne & Hannah are much dissatisfied one with another and hence jealousy, bickering and strife is the result." In an effort to make peace, he "removed Hannah to another house." Even so, David wrote, "Her conduct becomes more and more unbearable and puts me to much trouble." Not knowing how to make things right, David resorted to harsh, juvenile tactics: "I absent myself sometimes for weeks," he said, "then she craves forgiveness."[5]

Richard Ballantyne earnestly desired the happiness of his wives but felt he constantly fell short in pleasing them. "How delicate is the position of a man in plural marriage who loves his wives and who in turn is loved by them," he bemoaned. "Every move he makes, in his relation or intercourse with them, is an arrow that pierces deep into the heart of one or other. Even his very looks and thoughts are read; true, often misinterpreted to mean partiality for one at the expense of the other, be he ever so fair and good in his intentions. How difficult his Situation! What can he do to please them all? In trying to solve this question his difficulties only increase."[6]

Looking back over his married life, polygamist John J. Esplin concluded, "It wasn't meant for all men to have two wives and maybe I wasn't one of 'em. It's hard on a man that's kind of nervous. More than he can stand having to worry about them and seeing that everything is all right."[7] In a letter to her aunt, Mary Jane Mount Tanner observed, "I have told you men's lives were not strewn with roses in these much married relations. If women was all they wanted they could buy or steal them as others did and save themselves so much trouble."[8]

In contrast, some men found plural marriage more harmonious than expected. Oluf Larsen recorded that he and his wife

> knew the word of God [regarding polygamy] was true and that obedience would be attended with blessings. We also realized the trials and trouble that would follow obedience. We had examples before us on every hand. We finally concluded it would not be right to shrink from the duty any longer. My wife conveyed the idea to a girl working for us by the name of Amalia Anderson. She was glad and accepted the offer. . . . We lived together in the same house, ate at the same table and had peace and happiness in our family—even more than I had anticipated.[9]

Autonomy of Wives

A sense of independence from one's spouse became a hallmark of polygamous partnerships, especially for women. "In polygamy the man's interests are scattered," wrote plural wife Annie Clark Tanner. Women who "carry the whole responsibility of rearing a large family, are made capable by what is forced upon them," she said. "Naturally, these experiences give . . . a certain independence in attitude."[10] After adapting to running their own households, some women came to prefer distance from their husbands. Elizabeth Felt's husband, Joseph, rotated weekly among the homes of his three wives. "I was as glad to see his back as I was his face," Elizabeth recalled. "As I grew older, more and more I valued my independence and my personal freedom. And so did the other wives. We enjoyed having him come, but we enjoyed our liberty when he was gone."[11]

Some women thrived in their expanded autonomy. One wife described independence as a "great advantage" of plurality. By developing the "latent powers in woman's nature," she wrote, a wife becomes "the intelligent companion of her husband."[12]

At the same time, other women longed for an exclusivity with their husbands that they had lost or never received. "Plural marriage destroys the oneness of course," reflected first wife Mary Isabella Horne. "No one can ever feel the full weight of the curse till she enters into polygamy; it is a great trial of feelings, but not of faith." Yet, despite her "trial of feelings," Mary Isabella came to appreciate that she was "freer and can do herself individually things she never could have attempted before; and work out her individual character as separate from her husband." Still, she mourned the unitedness she felt would still be hers if her husband had remained a monogamist, "if God had willed it so."[13]

New Wives

As Mary Isabella's account indicated, the relationship between monogamous spouses often changed when another wife joined the family. For some women, heartache was most acute at the time a husband married a new wife.[14] Emily Ellingham Hart, first wife of James Hart, adapted slowly to her husband's marriage in 1861 to his second wife, Sabina Scheib. Eight months after the union, Emily recorded the anguish she still felt when her husband spent the night at Sabina's home: "I do pray earnestly for grace to bear all all things oh! my God thou alone knowest the trial this [is] to me[.] I often wonder how long are thy daughters to suffer this bitter trial to me worse than death yet if it is thy will I hope to be able to bear all thou requirest me to do."[15]

Welcoming new women into the family was difficult not only for first wives but for plural wives as well. Second wife Jane Charter Robinson Hindley grieved when her husband, John, decided to marry two additional women, writing in 1862, "I have wept night and day since this has been in antisapation; and the effect it has on me is most dreadfull to bear."[16] After meeting his two new wives, Jane wrote, "I cannot call them wives yet it seams so strange Oh what my feelings are this moment, life to me is not so joyous; it seems dark. My God help me in my weakness and forgive me if I falter in my duty and affection to him I love."[17]

For some couples, entering polygamy led to the dissolution of their own union. Caroline Chappell Woodward, a widow with one son, married Mathias Nelson (whom she called "Nelson") in 1861 as his first wife. The family of three settled in Tooele, Utah, and the newlyweds were unable to have children together. Caroline was strongly opposed to her husband practicing polygamy, but Mathias married twenty-nine-year-old Hedvig Christine Lundmark as a plural wife in 1878. Hedvig bore her first child in 1879, and Caroline moved to Butte, Montana. "I Love Nelson and it kills me for him to have another Woman," Caroline wrote to her son. "I Hate her so. I never can Live that Life again." Heartbroken, Caroline confided her impetus for leaving: "a man cannot Love two women and I knew he would think more of her with Children than he did of me and I could not live to see it[.]"[18] Caroline eventually divorced Mathias and remarried in Montana. About twenty-five years later, after the death of her husband in Montana, Caroline returned to Tooele to live near her son. There, she again associated with Mathias, and Caroline's granddaughter Bertha Nelson Tripp remembered that they "were like old sweethearts once more."[19]

Other Trials in Plural Marriage

Loneliness, neglect, and unmet expectations were particular trials in polygamous families. Frequent separation from one's spouse could be agonizingly lonely. Missing her absent husband, Emma Mecham Nielson wrote in her diary, "My heart is so sore and who in all this world can heal it except my dear F. G. [husband Frihoff Godfrey] one word from his precious lips at this moment could do it; I love him as I do my own life; and when can I linger by his side as I once use[d] to."[20] A man with many wives could also feel lonely, as though he did not quite belong anywhere. Although David Candland had three other wives living when his first wife died, he wrote of intense "lonesomeness" without her.[21]

Emmeline B. Wells, fifth Relief Society general president and editor of the newspaper the *Woman's Exponent*, was the seventh wife of Daniel H. Wells, a member of the First Presidency. She ached for her husband's presence, remembering "only the coming and going and parting at the door, the joy when he came the sorrow when he went as though all the light died out of my life."[22] Feeling the grief of neglect after two decades of marriage, Emmeline confided to her diary, "O if my husband could only love me even a little and not seem so perfectly indifferent to any sensation of that kind, he cannot know the craving of my nature, he is surrounded with love on every side, and I am cast out O my poor aching heart where shall it rest its burden, only on the Lord, only to Him can I look every other avenue seems closed against me."[23]

Martha Hughes married Angus Cannon as his fourth wife in 1884. She was forced to hide on the underground and sought refuge in England in 1886. After her return from England, she was unable to have the focused affection from her husband that she craved, and she became disillusioned. He had married two wives after Martha, so a total of six demanded his attention. She wrote to her friend, "My anticipations of happy associations with *loved* ones after my long exile were altogether overdrawn. . . . Look long and wisely before *you* choose a life *companion*, for tis deathly martyrdom to be linked to one who understands you not, and appreciates you less."[24]

Love between Husband and Wife

In 1873, Elizabeth Kane wrote, "I can only realize a wife's being contented to have her husband married to another if she has ceased to care for him herself, so that it is a matter of indifference to her where his affections are."[25] Some women coped with polygamy by doing just that: stifling love for their husbands. Vilate Murray Kimball, first wife of Heber C. Kimball, reportedly counseled an unhappy plural wife to "lay aside wholly all interest or thought in what her husband was doing while he was away from her" and be as "pleased to see him when he came in as she was pleased to see any friend."[26]

But love was not always lost, nor did it turn to indifference. Elizabeth Kane observed one Latter-day Saint couple in a polygamous arrangement and reflected, "There is something in [Maggie and Hugh McDiarmid's] manner to each other which, if they were not Mormons, would gladden the heart of an old novel reader like myself as a proof that after twenty years of wedlock; there could still be married lovers."[27]

Was it possible for a husband to have several wives and love each one? Esther Anderson Huntsman, a child of polygamists, asked her father that question. She said, "He always answered by asking me if a woman could love more than one child."[28] Letters between Parley P. Pratt and his tenth wife, Ann Agatha, testify to their passionate feelings for one another, even in the midst of his long absences in Church service. In a letter to Agatha, Parley effused that she was "dearer to me than my own hearts blood."[29] And she reassured him, "My love for you is boundless, my affection lasting as my soul, and my whole heart is as warm and unchangeable to you as always and will be while I have a being."[30] In her later reminiscences, she recalled Parley's ability to ardently love his wives as the "beloved of his bosom," and they deeply loved him in return.[31]

When Silas D. Smith married his second wife, Maria Bushman, he felt his capacity to love increase rather than divide in two. He said, "The same love burned in my heart for Maria as ever came in the love affairs with [my first wife] Ellen; that does not mean that I loved Ellen less nor Maria less. The heart of man grows and expands with knowledge and understanding of the correctness of the plural wife system. . . . That pure sincere love has always burned in my soul, and I thank my Heavenly Father for it."[32]

Many plural spouses found a bond of love, even if it took time to develop. For Laura Moffett, the second wife of Frederick William Jones, the connection came quietly and without ardor. Frederick was very much in love with his first wife, Elnora, and in all the years of their marriage, Laura felt that Frederick "never came to fully love me," but, she recorded poignantly, "I came, as he grew to love the children, to have a place in his heart."[33]

Emmeline B. Wells's relationship with her husband finally blossomed after thirty-seven years of marriage. Emmeline described feeling "more like lovers than husband and wife."[34] Upon his death just one year later, she mused, "Such intense love he has manifested towards me of late years. Such a remarkable change from the long ago—when I needed him so much more."[35]

Andrew J. Hansen and his third wife, Mary Christensen, hardly knew each other when they married. "I could not help but respect my husband as a good man, but for a long time I could not love him as he deserved," Mary wrote. "But gradually as the years have come and gone the change has come. . . . The dreams of happiness which I dreamed in my youth have been more than realized but not in the way that I looked for it to come. It has come about in the Lord's own way and I am really very happy."[36]

CHAPTER 11

RELATIONSHIPS AMONG WIVES

"While we had human nature to contend with, we worked and prayed . . . [to] learn to love each other."
—Lorena Washburn Larsen, 1939

A woman's experience of plural marriage was profoundly affected by her relationship with her sister wife or wives. These relationships led to the success of some marriages and the failure of others. Some wives lived together in the same household, while others lived apart and never knew each other well. Some were enemies; others, friends.

Receiving the support of the first wife helped to begin a plural union on the right footing. Most prospective plural wives were sensitive to the emotional pain that existing wives might experience when a new wife entered the family. Thus, some potential brides directly approached the first wife to assess her feelings before considering a marriage proposal from her husband. The following is correspondence between prospective plural bride Ida Hunt and David K. Udall's first wife, Eliza Luella ("Ella") in 1882. Wrote Ida:

> I cannot allow the matter [of plural marriage] to go farther, without first having received some assurance of your willingness to such a step being taken. . . . I believe in this matter, it is not only your right, but your imperative duty to state plainly any objections you may have in your feelings, and I beg you will not hesitate to do so, for I promise you I shall not be offended, but on the contrary, shall

> thank you for it all my life, . . . for, unless it meets with your approval, I shall never listen to another word on the subject.[1]

Nearly two months later, Ida received Ella's response:

> I have felt unable to reply sooner, and hardly feel equal to the task now. The subject in question is one which has caused me a great amount of pain and sorrow, more perhaps than you would imagine, yet I feel (as I have done from the beginning) that if it is the will of the Lord, I am perfectly willing to try to endure it; and trust it will be overruled for the best good of all. My feelings are such that I cannot write but briefly on this subject.[2]

Ida and David married shortly thereafter. Sorrow-driven tension with Ella, coupled with Ida's need to go on the underground, made married life especially challenging for Ida. Over time, the wives grew to appreciate each other. Ida continued to find joy in her family, but she also experienced difficulty, and circumstances necessitated that she build much of her life apart from her husband.

Jealousy and Heartbreak

One of the most common causes for tension between wives was jealousy. "It is natural not to like to see another loved by the object of our devotion," wrote Emily Spencer in the *Woman's Exponent* in 1878, "[but] by indulging in this miserable feeling [we] repel the love which we might enjoy."[3]

One woman who tried desperately to love her sister wife was Adelia Wilcox Hatton, a widow with three young children. Gideon D. Wood asked Adelia to become his second wife in 1854, shortly after she arrived in Utah. "I believed in the principle," she wrote. "[I] did not see what better I could do so I concluded to except his offer." Gideon's first wife, Hannah, "did not seem very well pleased but I thought that time would remove that feeling for I was determand to do all I could to gain her good will, but this is not so easaley done. After all a woman and three children being added to a famaley all at once is a big responsibility added to them[,] and a specley a woman coming in as a wife makes a grand difference, I can assure you if the first wife is opposed to you coming."

After two years of trying to improve her relationship with Hannah, Adelia felt only resentment in return. "I knew that my self an[d] children wher [were] looked upon as intruders," she said, "so I concluded to leave and told [Gideon] so. He tride to persuade me to stay and made many good promises to me if I would and the way he felt it almost overcame me. I fasted and prayed for three days and nights and still I could not change my mind." Adelia concluded, "No matter how good a man may be," if "his wife or wives live in open rebellion to him. . . . I do not beleave he can do any thing for them."[4] Adelia and Gideon divorced in 1856.

Finding Sisterhood

Maintaining Peace

Maintaining peace in a relationship with a sister wife sometimes required patience and self-restraint, as well as constant remembrance of *why* one had entered the order of plural marriage. Lorena Washburn Larsen lived with her husband's first wife for seven years of her marriage. "In all that time," wrote Lorena, "we never quarreled—not once, but I cannot say that we didn't sometimes feel like it; but we had gone into that order of marriage because we fully believed God had commanded it, and while we had human nature to contend with, we worked and prayed for strength to overcome selfishness and greed and live on a higher plain, learn to love each other, or there would never be happiness in our hearts and homes."[5]

Knowing the significance of compatibility between wives, one young woman waited to marry polygamously until she found a family in which, she stated, "I loved the woman as well as I loved the man."[6] Polygamy amplified the need to subdue selfish tendencies and develop attributes to maintain family harmony. Before her marriage as a third wife, Martha Cragun Cox received the advice to "speak no words when angry." Adapting to the dynamics of her new plural home provoked her "hot Irish temper," but she eventually acquired the self-discipline to hold her tongue and, as a result, created deeply meaningful kinships with her sister wives.[7]

Mary Woolley Chamberlain, her husband's sixth and youngest wife, seemed to step into a home where her co-wives had already weathered storms with human nature and had been refined by the process. She recorded beautifully in her biography, "Right here I want to pay a tribute of love and appreciation to those wives, than whom a better set of women never lived. If they ever had any ill feeling or jealousy toward me, it was locked in their own hearts, and never came to the surface, for they have always treated me with the greatest love and respect. I love them as dearly as my own sisters, and there is nothing I would not do to help them if I could."[8]

One way of defusing conflict between wives—or preventing it from the beginning—was to maintain a separate home for each wife. It became more common for sister wives to live apart as the century progressed, especially during the raids of the 1880s. Not surprisingly, physical distance brought greater peace to many women, but it also diminished the close relationships others had cultivated and deeply valued.

Forging Bonds

The sisterhood that some plural wives experienced was considered one of polygamy's blessings, even amid its difficulties. Some wives developed deep bonds through shared hardship. Helen Marr Clark married Thomas Callister as his second wife in Nauvoo. They were among the earliest Saints to arrive in Utah. Helen said of her sister wife, Caroline, "Together we trod the trackless wilds to reach these then sterile valleys; together we battled the hardships of the 'first year.' . . . Through those trying scenes ties closer than those of sister hood bound us together and the principle of plural marriage was firmly planted in our souls."[9]

Two sister wives described their relationship as "a closer tie than could be maintained between the most intimate friends."

They explained, "In our home, each of us has a friend whose interests are identical with her own, who can share all the joys and troubles of the family, and to whom she can impart her feelings regarding its head without fear of violating that sacred confidence which may not be shared with any outside friend."[10] Another pair of polygamous wives expressed "the comfort, to a simple family, that there was in having two wives to lighten the labors and duties of the household."[11]

Elizabeth Macdonald observed that, "A great deal of good can be done in a family of many wives" when they were united.[12] With the support of their sister wives, some women were able to expand their skills and pursue interests outside of the home. Ellis Reynolds Shipp's three sister wives made it possible for her to attend the Woman's Medical College of Pennsylvania from 1875 to 1877 by helping to finance her studies and care for her children. Ellis left her three young sons in the primary care of her "beloved sister Mary." "It was She," wrote Ellis, "my husbands youngest wife who made this effort possible for me, in whom I trusted most implicitly! & will ever love eternally!"[13] After Ellis returned as one of the first female medical doctors in Utah, she safely delivered more than six thousand babies and helped to establish the School of Nursing and Obstetrics, training over six hundred midwives.[14]

Some wives made profound sacrifices for each other. In 1867, Peter Nielsen recorded such an act in his journal: "My wife Hulda gave birth to a son at 8:30 a.m. . . . Hulda gave him to my wife Marie that she might have him as her son, as if she herself had given birth to him. Hulda did this [in] as much as Marie had only one son 16 years old. This made Marie rejoice very much; may the Lord bless this act and all my family and everything under my care is my prayer in the name of Jesus Christ. Amen."[15] Incredibly, this was not an isolated incident; giving one's own baby to a childless sister wife occurred in other families, although it was not commonplace.

One of the most significant roles a woman in plural marriage could assume was at the death of a sister wife who still had young children. In that scenario, many women stepped forward to raise a sister wife's children as their own. Zina D. H. Young, wife of Brigham Young, raised the four young children of her sister wife Clarissa Ross Young after Clarissa's untimely death. Phoebe Ann Covington Pace was nineteen when she married John Ezra Pace in 1877 as his second wife. As the years passed, two of John's three wives passed away. Between her own twelve children and those of her sister wives, Phoebe raised nineteen children.[16] While this is an unusual example, many records honor sister wives who raised children after their mothers had died.

In the best situations, sister wives became true sisters in spirit, sharing with one another the most intimate of life's experiences: birth and death, hardship and prosperity, and the pains and joys of learning and growth. Through years of shared experiences, deep bonds often developed. Martha Cragun Cox shared a home with her two sister wives and their children before the Raid forced them to separate. She wrote, "To me it is a joy to know that we laid the foundation of a life to come while we lived in that plural marriage, that we three who loved each other more than sisters, children of one mother love, will go hand in hand together down through all eternity. That knowledge is worth more to me than gold and more than compensates for all the sorrow I have ever known."[17]

In Retrospect

After decades of living in plurality, many women reflected upon the lessons they learned from their experiences. For some, the memories were painful; Agatha Walker McAllister wrote in 1944, "I am glad those old polygamous times are over. I don't like to think about them."[18] Many other women reflected positively on their experiences in polygamy—in spite of inner conflicts and challenges—and commonly coupled their conclusions with statements of faith. Sarah Barnes Layton reflected, "With all I have passed through I have never regretted that I received [the principle of plural marriage] in my younger days. I know that if we are true and faithful that principle will lead us on to exaltation and give us eternal lives in the kingdom of God. It is worth all the sacrifice any of us can make in this life."[19]

Ruth May Fox said, "I believed in [plural marriage], in the divinity of it, in the blessings it would bring. As a principle it will degrade or elevate and if lived rightly it will develop nobility of character and conquer selfishness, bringing out the good in people, or will do the opposite."[20]

Women often valued polygamy for who it helped them to become—not because it was easy, but because it was hard. Elizabeth Macdonald spoke plainly, "I do not wish to have it understood that I have had no trials in this Order. I have had many; and now am by no means sorry that I had them. I am thankful that in my trials I have not been overpowered; they have been very profitable to me, and have helped me to be a far better woman than I otherwise should be. The experience I have gained, and the self control I have attained is of more value to me than all I could possibly have obtained by avoiding it."[21]

Romania B. Pratt Penrose stated, "Were [plural marriage] lived according to the great and grand aim of its author, though it be a fiery furnace at some period of our life, it will prove the one thing needful to cleanse and purify our inmost soul of selfishness, jealousy and other mundane attributes which seem to lie closest to the citadel of life." Because one's soul was refined by this fiery furnace, she believed that one would be prepared to "enter and remain in the celestial Kingdom of our Father."[22]

Many early Saints who practiced plural marriage felt the same inner struggle as these women and, like them, developed a "nobility of character" in living a life that polygamy redefined.

CHAPTER 12

FAMILY RELATIONSHIPS

"When it was lived at its best,
it was truly a divine principle."
—Elizabeth Mineer Felt, 1937

Relationships within a polygamous family tree branched widely to include husbands and wives, wives and sister wives, children and parents, children and sister wives, children and siblings, and children and half-siblings. Polygamists shared common challenges, but the quality of family relationships gave individuals dramatically different experiences. Three significant variables that affected relationships included family living arrangements, cooperation among sister wives, and the presence of the father in family life. Exploring these few essential variables in a variety of polygamous living situations gives greater clarity to the range of experiences within plural households.

Family Living

The home life of polygamists was largely affected by living arrangements. Plural families were often large and thriving, and for those husbands, wives, and children who shared the same home, it could mean occasional mayhem. The daily trenches of raising a plural family—just like any family—were not seamless, serene scenes. Letters and journals carry tones familiar to many families today, but perhaps theirs were enhanced by the number of women and children in a household.

In 1855, Artimesia Snow, the first of four wives of Apostle Erastus Snow, wrote to her absent husband:

> You often ask how we enjoy ourselves[.] we enjoy ourselves as well as we can under the existing circumstances[.] we have a large family of little children and many different kinds[;] it is not very pleasant having so many kinds of children and so many different mistresses[.] if they all had one master or mistress it would be better[.] I become more and more satisfied every day of my life that it is no way to bring up children and I think that you would be convinced of that fact if you were at home a few evenings from sunset till dark and hear the music of the four babies[—] saying nothing of the others to join in and help them a little[.] we often wish you were hear [here] to hear them but we will try and stand it till you come home and then we will poke you up with hot blocks.[1]

While both men and women struggled to juggle their demanding responsibilities, many families found that a polygamous household actually had its benefits. In the Cox home, plural wife Martha Cragun Cox recorded, "We had our work so systematized and so well ordered that we could with ease do a great deal. One would for a period superintend the cooking and kitchen work with the help of the girls, another make beds and sweep, another comb and wash all the children." Household tasks such as sewing, shopping, laundry, and cooking were divided according to talents and tastes. "We had in our home an almost perfect United Order," Martha recalled. "We enjoyed many privileges that single wiferey never knew."[2]

Raising Children

In referring to her preference for "one master or mistress" in child-rearing, Artimesia Snow may have been hinting at the challenge of different parenting styles within the same household. In a letter to her husband, Apostle Joseph F. Smith, Edna Lambson Smith related a confrontation she had with her sister wife Sarah about Sarah's tendency to "let her baby screem

Courtesy Church History Library

President Joseph F. Smith with his five wives and children on his sixtieth birthday, 1898

from morning till night." Sarah responded, "I don't care if I do let him cry." To Sarah, it was more important to "get her work [done even] if he did cry."[3]

The chaotic scenes of daily life faded over time, and for many, the positive memories outlived the daily stresses. Thirty years later, Julina Lambson Smith—a sister wife of Edna and Sarah—remembered those early days with idyllic fondness. Reflecting on the period when she shared a home with her two sister wives and their husband, she wrote, "Even now I can hear the laughter of our children as they played about us before being kissed, and tucked in their beds. There, too, I can see the evening picture of three tired but happy mothers, often busy with kneeless stockings, seatless trousers or other articles of clothing needing buttons or stitches; or with, perhaps, something good to read or ideas to exchange."[4]

Teaching and raising children could be divided labor as well. Joseph W. Pratt, a child of polygamous parents, recounted that his mother taught school while her sister wife cared for the children, cooked, kept house, and, in Joseph's words, "was just like a mother to me."[5] Annie Richardson Johnson enjoyed "the benefit of the talents of all of [her mothers]. If one could sing and play the piano, they would teach the others."[6]

The Father's Presence

The presence or absence of the husband and father could cast "sunshine or shade" on his families.[7] As both Artimesia and Edna's letters imply, the frequent absence of the husband was a common burden of polygamous wives. The independence women often found in plural marriage applied particularly to the raising of children and running a household. Church responsibilities, missions, employment, or distantly located wives and children pulled husbands away for long periods. For these reasons, Emeline Grover Rich, fifth wife of Apostle Charles C. Rich, reflected in her diary that "[I] Have had but little [help] in the rearing of and providing for my family—[I] have [had] as it were, to take the part of father and mother." When Charles came, she recorded, he was "like a visitor."[8]

Like Emeline, many wives shouldered the responsibilities of single mothers. Ten years after Emma Mecham and Frihoff Godfrey Nielson married in 1877, Frihoff married his second wife, Mary Ellen Everett. The two wives lived about fifty miles apart in New Mexico, and Frihoff was gone for months at a time running Mary Ellen's farm or fulfilling Church duties in St. Johns, Arizona. Emma had to adapt to caring for their young children on her own and running a household without her husband's physical and emotional support. Several months after her husband's second marriage, Emma recorded in her diary, "After getting my precious little ones in bed I took a walk in the moonlight all the while wondering where my precious FG was. . . . How pleased I would be if he would step in [and] administer to our wants, soothe the cries of my four little ones and do a fathers part; how their little hearts would leap with joy at first site; they have looked forward to the time (so long) that they would see their Pa that they begin to think they have no Pa. I feel heart broken my self."[9] Emma, of necessity, braved significant life experiences alone. Three years later, she wrote, "I gave birth to a baby girl while my husband was at St. John's Ariz. It was a cold night and no one with me but my little children."[10]

In what became a microcosmic matriarchal society in some homes, mother and child developed particularly strong bonds. In fact, mothers were advised to take comfort "wholly in her children" and not fret about her husband in his absence.[11] Without a husband in whom to confide, a mother often turned to her children for emotional support. Ellen Pratt McGary clung to her six-month-old baby: "She is so much company for me while her father is gone I don't know how I should live without her."[12] Olive Andelin Potter wrote, "I have worshiped my children all my life, as I have had no husband to love so all my love has been for them."[13] Archie L. Jenkins, a child of polygamous parents, said, "We respected Father but he never gave us a chance to really love him as non-polygamist families seemed to enjoy with a father patriarch dedicated to one single family."[14]

Absences were difficult for husbands, too, and they often struggled to meet the complicated needs of their large families. Away from his family for employment, Hiram Clawson addressed a letter to his three "dear wives." "I feel pretty blue I can tell you," he wrote, reflecting on his loneliness without them. "I shall be glad Enough I can tell you when the words comes for me to leave. . . . Hoping that I shall be with you in a few days."[15]

On the opposite end of the spectrum, when the legal climate allowed plural families to live together or very near one another, the father had greater opportunity to be an active presence in the lives of each of his wives and children. Henry W. Naisbitt reflected in 1885 that "no better time have I had in thirty years of married life than when I had three wives given me of God, and occupying but one habitation. The power of God was in that home; the spirit of peace was there, the spirit of intelligence was there; and we had our ever present testimony that God recognized the patriarchal order."[16]

Juanita Brooks, born in 1898 to monogamous parents, grew up in the Latter-day Saint community of Bunkerville, Nevada, and recalled her observations of a polygamous family who shared daily life with one another:

> My most intimate knowledge of the every-day living of [polygamy] came from my best girl friend, who was a polygamous child about my age. For the first eighteen years of my life I lived across the street from her. . . . I had never considered her family as being different from mine, except that it was larger. There was nothing secret, nothing unusual at all about it. The wives lived in the same block; between them was the family granary and tool shop, in the center of the block the corrals and haystack. . . . Uncle Tom [the polygamous father] spent one night at one home and the next at the other, regularly, as long as I knew him, unless there were sickness at one home or the other, when he stayed to help with it. . . .
>
> Somehow he kept order among them all, and co-operation to the extent that his haystacks were larger, his granaries better filled, and his children better dressed than any of his neighbors. No one saw anything unusual in the fact that when he went to church or to any public gathering he always took both wives and always walked between them. The children were all treated alike; his pride in them and his tendency to brag publicly of them became something of a town joke. When he died . . . every child was present at the funeral service and I have never seen more genuine evidence of respect anywhere.[17]

The Spirit of Polygamy

What was it like to live in a polygamous family? Generalizations are impossible. In addition to the three variables explored here, other variables—such as the time period in which a couple married; financial, social, and ecclesiastical status; community of residence; number of wives in the family and a woman's numerical wife position; and the level of religious commitment in a home—created a wealth of possible dynamics.

People did find happiness in plural families. Plural wife M. E. Talmage believed, "God has blessed me for honoring that law [of plurality]; I am satisfied, contented, and happy in my home. I love my husband, his family and my children."[18] After a lifetime of observing plural families, Elizabeth Felt noted: "When people had what I call the spirit of polygamy they were happy and they raised good and happy families. . . . It was a hard principle to live, but when it was lived at its best, it was truly a divine principle."[19]

CONCLUSION

WHAT DOES POLYGAMY MEAN FOR LATTER-DAY SAINTS TODAY?

"Plural marriage, as it was practiced, served its purpose."

—Elder Quentin L. Cook, 2020

Now, over a century removed from Joseph F. Smith's 1904 Second Manifesto, what does polygamy mean for members of The Church of Jesus Christ of Latter-day Saints today? The Gospel Topics Essays published on the official Church website suggest that the lasting effects of plural marriage were "the birth of large numbers of children within faithful Latter-day Saint homes," the availability of marriage to "virtually all who desired it," equalized wealth per capita, "ethnic intermarriages," and aid in uniting "a diverse immigrant population."[1] Polygamy provided a sense of group solidarity as Latter-day Saints saw themselves as separate from other religious sects, a "peculiar people" (1 Pet. 2:9). Indeed, in its purpose to "raise up seed unto [the Lord]," polygamy was remarkably effective (Jacob 2:30). Research suggests that 20 percent of living Church members descend from those who practiced polygamy.[2]

When plural marriage was discontinued, polygamists, too, reflected on its purpose and many believed it had been fulfilled. Said one plural wife, "Polygamy has served its day. We helped to populate Utah and to make it possible for every woman to become a mother. . . . We have served our purpose and polygamy has gone."[3]

Present-day Church teachings have made clear that the

"standard of the Lord's people is monogamy" between one man and one woman, and the approximate fifty-year period during which Church members practiced polygamy was a rare exception to that standard.[4] Today, Church members no longer practice polygamy, even in countries where polygamy is legal.

Many modern Latter-day Saints still question the principle of plural marriage and wonder why it was practiced. Some have feared that they, too, will be required to live polygamously in this life or in the next. It is natural to wonder how our polygamous past and the teachings of past leaders will affect our future.

Messages from Church Leaders Today

It is essential to remember that the words of modern prophets outweigh those of past prophets.[5] The following are messages about plural marriage from Church leaders today:

Apostle Quentin L. Cook, reflecting on nineteenth-century polygamy, shared that "plural marriage, as it was practiced, served its purpose. We should honor those Saints, but that purpose has been accomplished." Elder Cook acknowledged that "there are unanswered questions. But I want you to know that we have a loving Heavenly Father who has a perfect plan, that His plan is one of happiness, and that we have a Savior who did everything for us. We can trust in Them."[6]

In 2015, Elder Marcus B. Nash clarified that some members "inaccurately read" portions of Doctrine and Covenants 132, "leading them to believe that plural marriage is a necessary prerequisite for exaltation in the eternal realm. This, however, is not supported in the revelations." He further stated, "By setting forth the law of eternal marriage in the context of a monogamous marriage, the Lord makes plain that the blessings of exaltation, extended to each man and each woman who worthily enters into the covenant of eternal marriage performed by proper priesthood authority, are independent of whether that marriage is plural or monogamous [see D&C 131; 132:4–7, 15–25]."[7]

The Place of Polygamy in Eternity

President Dallin H. Oaks has noted that we have little scriptural information about the "conditions and relationships" in the kingdoms of glory in the afterlife, and this applies directly to questions about plural marriage in the hereafter.[8] The Church readily admits that "the precise nature of these relationships in the next life is not known, and many family relationships will be sorted out in the life to come."[9]

Unfortunately, unknowns have too often been answered with speculation and myths, creating undue fear and angst within some Saints. Among the details we do know about the afterlife are that the work of salvation continues there; ordinances performed on earth have effect in the spirit world; the sealing power can bind, as well as loosen, relationships; and agency, or freedom of choice, is an eternal principle.

Although Latter-day Saints no longer perform living polygamous marriages, the Church has never renounced the doctrine of plural marriage. The revelation on eternal and plural marriage is still canonized as Doctrine and Covenants 132, and eternal sealings, be they nineteenth-century plural marriages or monogamous marriages, are still considered binding in the next world. Remnants of the practice still exist in Latter-day Saint temples as men who have been sealed to a wife now deceased are able to be sealed to another, living woman, granting them more than one wife eternally. A living woman, on the other hand, is not allowed to be eternally sealed to more than one man, even if her husband is deceased. In 1998, the Church introduced a policy that after a woman's death, she could be sealed to more than one man by proxy—a reflection of the attitude that unknowns will be sorted out in the hereafter.[10]

Unanswered questions about polygamy in the afterlife are painful for some Church members and no doubt reflect similar tensions that nineteenth-century Latter-day Saints wrestled with. How did they answer those questions with faith? Ultimately, nineteenth-century Saints received answers individually, based on their unique circumstances. Not all chose to live polygamously, nor were they required to do so.

Self-Examination

Polygamy forces us to examine ourselves and our belief in the nature of God. Is He a God of justice and mercy? Does He desire our eternal happiness as daughters and sons, to exalt and bless equally and liberally? Eliza R. Snow affirmed in 1869 that "there is not a wish or desire that the Lord has implanted in our hearts in righteousness but will be realized."[11] As scripture and modern Church leaders confirm, heartfelt desires for oneness with a single companion will be honored and, when bound worthily by the eternal marriage covenant, honored with exaltation.

For those faithful Saints who chose plural marriages in the nineteenth century, it is my belief that the righteous yearnings of their hearts will also be realized. "Every tear" they may have shed as a result of their obedience to this principle "will eventually be returned a hundredfold with tears of rejoicing and gratitude."[12] There is no sorrow in our Heavenly Parents' great plan of happiness.

God's View of the Family

What can our polygamous past teach us about our Heavenly Parents' view of the family? Perhaps it is both akin to and more expansive than our own. Carole M. Stephens, first counselor in the Relief Society general presidency (2012–17), stated, "Earthly families all look different," but, "we each belong to and are needed in the family of God." We are "sealed to Him as part of His eternal family," and His plan "is a plan to unite His children—His family—with Him."[13] The sealing ordinance binds not only a husband, wife, and their children to each other but also unites them with God. Our divine destiny is to gather around our Heavenly Parents again as exalted beings, united together as one family, for this is His work and His glory (Moses 1:39).

The Legacy of Plural Marriage

In 1909, Sarah Comstock, a writer for *Collier's Magazine*, visited St. George, Utah. Not a Latter-day Saint herself, Sarah talked with many aged residents who had settled that area, many of whom were polygamists. She listened to their stories and summarized her observations of plural marriage, concluding that even with the variety of attitudes toward plural marriage, "the belief among all the old-school Latter-Day Saints and many of the younger ones [is] that it is right; and that unswerving belief has made polygamy possible. . . . Now that they have been through their ordeal, they are passing into an old age made content by faith in the glory soon to be theirs."[14]

When I first began my journey studying polygamy, I was angry by what I saw as injustice that God required such a difficult principle to be lived by these faithful, tried people. But as I studied the personal writings, stories, and testimonies of polygamists, accepting them on their own terms, I found peace. To me, Sarah Comstock's observation summarizes what made polygamy possible for nineteenth-century Saints: the belief that it was right. The practice could never have been sustained for a half-century by compulsion, manipulation, or simple sexual desire. Those who set the foundation of the Latter-day Saint faith were not two-dimensional superheroes, as they are sometimes portrayed, but they were complex, strong, intelligent, full-bodied kingdom-builders who were willing to leave loved ones, wealth, comfort, and native countries for what they believed to be true. This same willingness drove them to accept polygamy, a practice they accepted as a commandment of God instituted in their time, for His unique purposes.

So, must modern Latter-day Saints share the same conviction as early Saints that polygamy was "right"? As early as 1856, Saints who desired to receive ordinances in the temple, such as the endowment and sealing, were asked a series of questions to determine their commitment to the gospel and their worthiness to receive those sacred ordinances and blessings. Among those questions, they were asked if they had a belief in "the plurality [plural marriage]."[15] Although they were not required to practice polygamy, belief in it was a measure of faithfulness before ordinances were received. This affirmation has not been required since that time.[16] The essential convictions of Latter-day Saints are defined in today's temple recommend questions—such as having faith in God the Father, a testimony of Jesus Christ as our Savior and Redeemer, and supporting and sustaining our leaders today.[17] Plural marriage is not a commandment in our day, and a belief in it is not required to be a faithful, believing Church member. What is essential is that we live the gospel of Jesus Christ *today* and make and keep sacred covenants *today*.

We can gain strength from our polygamous past. How? We can talk about it. We can discard shame and embarrassment about the practice. We can make room for complexity, knowing that each Saint had a story: some had positive and others negative experiences living plurally. We can share the stories of polygamous Saints and find meaning in their devotion. We can allow their faith to invigorate our own resolve to make difficult choices and sacrifices for the gospel's sake. We can sit in the discomfort of not having all of the answers and accept the reality that, even in important questions about polygamy, the answers may not be known right now. We can leave the burden of choice with the nineteenth-century Saints; they've already borne it. They knew their lives and situations better than we do. We can trust in God, as they did, and make and keep our own sacred covenants.

Polygamy was a difficult principle to live. What is remarkable, though, is that so many Saints infused plural marriage with love, compassion, and forgiveness, transcending earthly circumstances through the power of faith. Although we may never fully understand the principle, the nineteenth-century practice of plural marriage by members of The Church of Jesus Christ of Latter-day Saints is a legacy of faith to honor, a foundation of sacrifice to acknowledge, a history to gain strength from, and a bright testimony borne in the lives of those who practiced polygamy.

FURTHER READING

General Histories

Bringhurst, Newell G. and Craig L. Foster. *The Persistence of Polygamy*, 3 vols. Independence, MO: John Whitmer Books, 2010–15.

Daynes, Kathryn M. *More Wives Than One: Transformation of the Mormon Marriage System, 1840–1890*. Urbana and Chicago: University of Illinois Press, 2001.

Embry, Jessie L. *Mormon Polygamous Families: Life in the Principle*. Salt Lake City: University of Utah Press, 1987.

Hales, Brian C. *Joseph Smith's Polygamy*, 3 vols. Salt Lake City: Greg Kofford Books, 2013.

Hardy, B. Carmen. *Solemn Covenant: The Mormon Polygamous Passage*. Urbana and Chicago: University of Illinois Press, 1992.

Smith, Merina. *Revelation, Resistance and Mormon Polygamy: The Introduction and Implementation of the Principle, 1830–1853*. Logan: Utah State University Press, 2013.

Ulrich, Laurel Thatcher. *A House Full of Females: Plural Marriage and Women's Rights in Early Mormonism, 1835–1870*. New York: Alfred A. Knopf, 2017.

Van Wagoner, Richard S. *Mormon Polygamy: A History*. Salt Lake City: Signature Books, 1989.

Legal Issues and Polygamy

Flake, Kathleen. *Politics of American Religious Identity: The Seating of Senator Reed Smoot, Mormon Apostle*. Chapel Hill: University of North Carolina Press, 2004.

Gordon, Sarah Barringer. *The Mormon Question: Polygamy and Constitutional Conflict in Nineteenth-Century America*. Chapel Hill: University of North Carolina Press, 2002.

Websites

"Plural Marriage in Kirtland and Nauvoo"; "Plural Marriage and Families in Early Utah," Gospel Topics Essays, The Church of Jesus Christ of Latter-day Saints, https://www.churchofjesuschrist.org/study/manual/gospel-topics/essays.

Brian and Laura Harris Hales, Joseph Smith's Polygamy, www.josephsmithspolygamy.org.

NOTES

Abbreviations

The following abbreviations are used in the notes:

BYU L. Tom Perry Special Collections, Harold B. Lee Library, Brigham Young University, Provo, Utah
CHL Church History Library, The Church of Jesus Christ of Latter-day Saints, Salt Lake City
D&C Doctrine and Covenants
JD *Journal of Discourses*, 26 vols. (Liverpool: F. D. and S. W. Richards, 1855–86)
SLC Salt Lake City, Utah
WE *Woman's Exponent*

Introduction: Piecing Together Polygamy

1. "Kate and the Mormons," *Chicago Tribune*, June 6, 1886; John Taylor, "Hostility of the World to the Gospel," Feb. 12, 1882, *JD*, 26:95.
2. This information was collected in early- to mid-twentieth century and is assumed to reflect the general pattern of the nineteenth century. See George P. Murdock, *Ethnographic Atlas* (Pittsburgh: University of Pittsburgh Press, 1967); Miriam Koktvedgaard Zeitzen, *Polygamy: A Cross-Cultural Analysis* (Oxford and New York: Berg, 2008).
3. See Sarah M. S. Pearsall, *Polygamy: An Early American History* (New Haven: Yale University Press, 2019); Lawrence Foster, *Religion and Sexuality* (Urbana and Chicago: University of Illinois Press, 1984).

Chapter 1: Beginnings of Polygamy (1830–40)

1. See Nancy F. Cott, *Public Vows* (Cambridge, MA: Harvard University Press, 2000); Foster, *Religion and Sexuality*.
2. See Jennifer Reeder, *First: The Life and Faith of Emma Smith* (Salt Lake City: Deseret Book, 2021).
3. "Report of Elders Orson Pratt and Joseph F. Smith," *Millennial Star,* Dec. 16, 1878, 40:788.
4. Danel W. Bachman, "New Light on an Old Hypothesis," *Journal of Mormon History* 5 (1978): 19–32.
5. Joseph Smith, journal, Nov. 24, 1835, 49, www.josephsmithpapers.org; William G. Hartley, "Newel and Lydia Bailey Knight's Kirtland Love Story and Historic Wedding," *BYU Studies* 39, no. 4 (2000): 7–22; Kathleen Flake, "The Development of Early Latter-day Saint

Marriage Rites, 1831–53," *Journal of Mormon History* 41, no. 1 (Jan. 2015): 79–84.

6. "Fanny Alger," Church History Topics, www.churchofjesuschrist.org; *Saints*, 1:291–92, www.churchofjesuschrist.org; Richard Lyman Bushman, *Joseph Smith: Rough Stone Rolling* (New York: Vintage Books, 2007), 323–27. Primary evidence for this marriage relies on the following sources: Levi W. Hancock, Autobiography, ca. 1854, 63, CHL; Oliver Cowdery to Warren A. Cowdery, Jan. 21, 1838, Huntington Library, San Marino, CA; Minute Book 2, Apr. 12, 1838, 123–24, www.josephsmithpapers.org.
7. Marriage Record, *Indiana Marriages, 1811–2007*, www.familysearch.org; "Fanny Alger," Church History Topics.
8. Visions, Apr. 3, 1836 in Joseph Smith, Journal, 1835–36, 192–93, www.josephsmithpapers.org.
9. The Book of Common Prayer (New York: Auxiliary New York Bible and Common Prayer Book Society, 1823), 150.
10. For example, see Robert B. Thompson, "An Investigation of the Priesthood from the Scriptures," Oct. 5, 1840, CHL; Martha Jane Knowlton Coray, "Sermon 3[thd]," notebook, Aug. 13, 1843, 31–36, CHL; Wilford Woodruff, journal, Jan. 21 and Mar. 10, 1844, CHL.
11. Parley P. Pratt, *The Autobiography of Parley P. Pratt*, ed. Parley P. Pratt [Jr.] (Chicago: Law, King and Law, 1888), 329–30; Terryl L. Givens and Matthew J. Grow, *Parley P. Pratt* (New York: Oxford University Press, 2011), 203.

Chapter 2: Nauvoo Polygamy (1841–46)

1. Eliza R. Snow Smith, *Biography and Family Record of Lorenzo Snow* (SLC: Deseret News, 1884), 68–70.
2. Although polygamy is not condemned in the Bible, it *is* condemned in the Book of Mormon. See Jacob 2:23–35.
3. Most information on this period comes from later legal documents, reminiscences, or disaffected members of the Church.
4. See John Taylor, "Sermon in Honor of the Martyrdom," June 27, 1854, trans. LaJean P. Carruth, 7–8, CHL; Helen Mar [Kimball] Whitney, *Why We Practice Plural Marriage* (SLC: Juvenile Instructor Office, 1884), 56–59.
5. "Plural Marriage in Kirtland and Nauvoo," Gospel Topics Essays, www.churchofjesuschrist.org; Brian C. Hales, *Joseph Smith's Polygamy*, 3 vols. (SLC: Greg Kofford Books, 2013), 2:268–86; Todd Compton, *In Sacred Loneliness* (Salt Lake City: Signature Books, 1997).
6. Laurel Thatcher Ulrich, *A House Full of Females* (New York City: Alfred Knopf, 2017), 84n1.
7. Mary Fielding Smith, poem, n.d., CHL; Mary and Hyrum were sealed on May 29, 1843, and Mary acted as proxy while Hyrum was also sealed to Jerusha, his first wife, who had died. Hyrum married two plural wives in August 1843.

8. William Clayton, journals, vol. 1, Mar. 7, 1843, CHL.
9. Samuel M. Brown, "Early Mormon Adoption Theology and the Mechanics of Salvation," and Jonathan A. Stapley, "Adoptive Sealing Ritual in Mormonism," *Journal of Mormon History* 37, no. 2 (Summer 2011): 3–52, 53–117.
10. Benjamin F. Johnson to George F. Gibbs, Apr. 1903–Oct. 1911, 35, CHL; underlining in original.
11. Bushman, *Rough Stone Rolling*, 440. Linking both family and friends through the sealing ordinance later evolved to focus primarily on family relationships. Wilford Woodruff and George Q. Cannon, "The Law of Adoption," *Deseret Weekly*, Apr. 21, 1894.
12. "Plural Marriage in Kirtland and Nauvoo," Gospel Topics Essays, n24; Hales, *Joseph Smith's Polygamy*, 2:268–86; Compton, *In Sacred Loneliness*.
13. "Plural Marriage in Kirtland and Nauvoo," Gospel Topics Essays. According to one scholar, Joseph Smith was sealed to ten women under the age of twenty. Four were nineteen, three were seventeen, one was sixteen, one was fifteen or fourteen, and one was fourteen. In the mid–nineteenth century in the United States, the common age of marriage varied by region. In Joseph Smith's native New York, for example, 29.5 percent of young women married under the age of twenty in 1847, while in states such as South Carolina and Kentucky, young women often married during their teenage years, with around 40 percent of young women doing so in the 1850s. On the western frontier—of which Nauvoo, Illinois, was a part—early marriages were common. Nicholas L. Syrett, *American Child Bride* (Chapel Hill: University of North Carolina Press, 2016), Kindle edition; "Sealings to Young Brides," www.josephsmithspolygamy.org.
14. Helen Mar Kimball Whitney, autobiography, 1881, 1–2, CHL.
15. Brigham Young, "A Few Words of Doctrine," Oct. 8, 1861, 3, CHL; Compton, *In Sacred Loneliness*, 10–11, 17–18, 22–23; Hales, 3:195–96.
16. Lucy Walker Smith Kimball, affidavit, Dec. 17, 1902, CHL.
17. See Merina Smith, *Revelation, Resistance, and Mormon Polygamy*, (Logan: Utah State University Press, 2013), 75–76.
18. Because the Nauvoo Temple and the Saints' understanding of temple ceremonies were both incomplete, ordinances were not always performed in the temple or in the sequence now required. See Celestial Marriage Affidavits, CHL.
19. Temple Lot Transcript, Part 3, 105–6, 371, 384, questions 224–60, 480–84, 751–62, CHL; Malissa [Lott] Willes, affidavit, Aug. 4, 1893, CHL; Benjamin F. Johnson to George F. Gibbs, 1903 Apr.–Oct. 1911, 31–32, CHL; Lucy Walker Smith Kimball, affidavit, Dec. 17, 1902, CHL. For examples of eternity-only sealings, see Hales, *Joseph Smith's Polygamy*, 1:421–37; Helen Mar Kimball Whitney, autobiography, 1881, 1–2, CHL; John W. Wight, "Evidence from Zina D. Huntington-Young," *Saints Herald* 52 (Jan. 11, 1905): 29.
20. Whitney, autobiography, 1881, 2; J. Spencer Fluhman, "A Subject

that Can Bear Investigation," in *No Weapon Shall Prosper*, ed. Robert L. Millet (Provo, UT: Religious Studies Center; SLC: Deseret Book, 2011), 105–19.

21. Ugo A. Perego, "Using Science to Answer Questions from Latter-day Saint History: The Case of Josephine Lyon's Paternity," *BYU Studies Quarterly* 58, no. 4 (2019): 143–50; Ugo A. Perego, Natalie M. Myers, and Scott R. Woodward, "Reconstructing the Y-Chromosome of Joseph Smith," *Journal of Mormon History* 31 (Summer 2005): 70–88; Ugo A. Perego, Jane E. Ekins, and Scott R. Woodward, "Resolving the Paternities of Oliver N. Buell and Mosiah L. Hancock through DNA," *The John Whitmer Historical Association Journal* 28 (2008): 128–36.
22. Willes, affidavit, Aug. 4, 1893.
23. Compton, *In Sacred Loneliness*, 15. Joseph may have been sealed to as many as fourteen women with legal husbands. "Sealings to Legally Married Women," www.josephsmithspolygamy.org.
24. Hales, *Joseph Smith's Polygamy*, 1:421–37; "Plural Marriage in Kirtland and Nauvoo," Gospel Topics Essay, n30.
25. See Brian C. Hales, "Encouraging Joseph Smith to Practice Plural Marriage," *Mormon Historical Studies* 11, no. 2 (Fall 2010): 55–71.
26. Mary Elizabeth Rollins Lightner, statement, Feb. 8, 1902, CHL; Mary Elizabeth Rollins Lightner, "Mary Elizabeth Rollins," Utah State Historical Society, SLC; Marinda Nancy Johnson Hyde, statement, ca. 1880, CHL; Joseph F. Smith, "Correction," *Deseret Evening News*, Feb. 18, 1882.
27. Zina D. H. Young, autobiographical sketches 1, 1, CHL; Martha Sonntag Bradley and Mary Brown Firmage Woodward, *4 Zinas* (SLC: Signature Books, 2000), 113–14.
28. Compton, *In Sacred Loneliness*, chap. 4; "A Book of Proxey," no. 142, in Lyndon W. Cook, *Nauvoo Marriages Proxy Dealings, 1843–1846* (Provo, UT: Grandin Book, 2004), 178.
29. "Plural Marriage in Kirtland and Nauvoo," Gospel Topics Essays.
30. "Chauncy L. Higbee," *Nauvoo Neighbor*, May 29, 1844; Gary James Bergera, "John C. Bennett, Joseph Smith, and the Beginnings of Mormon Plural Marriage in Nauvoo," *John Whitmer Historical Association Journal* 25 (2005): 76–77.
31. "John C. Bennett's Spiritual Wifery," www.josephsmithspolygamy.org.
32. John C. Bennett, *The History of the Saints* (Boston: Leland and Whiting, 1842).
33. "Plural Marriage in Kirtland and Nauvoo," Gospel Topics Essays.
34. "Joseph Smith and Celestial Marriage," *Deseret Evening News*, May 20, 1886. See William Clayton, *An Intimate Chronicle: The Journals of William Clayton*, ed. George D. Smith (SLC: Signature Books, 1995), 10; "Polygamy Denials?" www.josephsmithspolygamy.org.
35. Jill Mulvay Derr, Carol Cornwall Madsen, Kate Holbrook, and Matthew J. Grow, eds., *The First Fifty Years of Relief Society* (SLC: Church Historian's Press, 2016), doc. 1.6.
36. Joseph Smith, journal, Oct. 5, 1843, [117], CHL; "City Council,

Regular Session, June 8th [and 10th], 1844," *Nauvoo Neighbor*, June 19, 1844.

37. "Reflections and Blessings, 16 and 23 August 1842," 164, www.josephsmithpapers.org.
38. Linda King Newell and Valeen Tippetts Avery, *Mormon Enigma* (Garden City, NY: Doubleday, 1984), 124.
39. Joseph Smith [III], "Last Testimony of Sister Emma," *Saints' Herald* 26 (Oct. 1, 1879): 289–90.
40. Emily Dow Partridge Smith Young, autobiography, 318, CHL; Emily Dow Partridge Young, "Incidents in the Life of a Mormon Girl," 186–87, CHL; Eliza Maria Partridge Lyman, affidavit, July 1, 1869, CHL; Emily Dow Partridge Young, affidavit, May 1, 1869, CHL; Lovina Walker, certificate, June 16, 1869, CHL.
41. Young, autobiography, 318; Emily Dow Partridge Young, "Autobiography," 2–3, CHL.
42. See Newell and Avery, *Mormon Enigma*; Ulrich, *House Full of Females*, 89–93.
43. William Clayton, affidavit, Feb. 16, 1874, 3, CHL.
44. William Victor Smith, *Textual Studies of the Doctrine and Covenants: The Plural Marriage Revelation* (SLC: Greg Kofford Books, 2018), chap. 8.
45. *Journals of William Clayton*, 110, 117.
46. Emma Smith, "Blessing," 1844, CHL. The location of the original is unknown.
47. Young, "Autobiography," Nov. 4, 1883, 4.
48. Joseph F. Smith, "Plural Marriage," July 7, 1878, *JD*, 20:29.
49. Ronald W. Walker, "Six Days in August: Brigham Young and the Succession Crisis of 1844," in *A Firm Foundation*, ed. David J. Whittaker and Arnold K. Garr (Provo, UT: Religious Studies Center; SLC: Deseret Book, 2011), 161–96; D. Michael Quinn, "The Mormon Succession Crisis of 1844," *BYU Studies* 16, no. 2 (1976): 1–44.
50. Gary James Bergera, "The Earliest Eternal Sealings for Civilly Married Couples Living and Dead," *Dialogue* 35, no. 3 (Fall 2002): 41–66.
51. "Plural Marriage in Kirtland and Nauvoo," Gospel Topics Essays; Mercy F. Thompson, Autobiographical Sketch, 7, CHL; Catherine P. Smith affidavit, Nov. 7, 1902, CHL.
52. See Brian C. Hales, "Joseph Smith's Plural Wives after the Martyrdom," *Mormon Historical Studies* 13, nos. 1–2 (2012): 55–68.
53. Jill Mulvay Derr, "The Lion and the Lioness: Brigham Young and Eliza R. Snow," *BYU Studies* 40, no. 2 (2001): 57; Leonard J. Arrington, *Brigham Young: American Moses* (New York: Alfred A. Knopf, 1985), 120–21.
54. "Plural Marriage in Kirtland and Nauvoo," Gospel Topics Essays.
55. George D. Smith, "Nauvoo Roots of Mormon Polygamy, 1841–46," *Dialogue* 27, no. 1 (Spring 1994): 29–32.
56. Lisle G. Brown, comp., *Nauvoo Sealings, Adoptions, and Anointings*

(SLC: Smith-Petit Foundation, 2006); Bergera, "Earliest Eternal Sealings."

57. Smith [III], "Last Testimony of Sister Emma," 289–90.
58. Inez Smith Davis, *The Story of the Church* (Independence, MO: Herald House, 1934).

Chapter 3: Polygamy in Transition (1846–47)

1. Glen M. Leonard, *Nauvoo* (SLC: Deseret Book, 2002); William Shepard, "Marshaled and Disciplined for War," *John Whitmer Historical Association Journal* 33, no. 2 (Fall/Winter 2013): 79–131.
2. Zina D. H. Young, in Edward W. Tullidge, *The Women of Mormondom* (New York: Tullidge and Crandall, 1877), 327.
3. "Iowa, LDS Communities In," *Encyclopedia of Mormonism* (New York: Macmillan, 1992), 698. Many Saints were also in St. Louis. Richard E. Bennett, *Mormons at the Missouri* (Norman: University of Oklahoma Press, 1987), 90.
4. Bennett, *Mormons at the Missouri*, 89.
5. Patty B. Sessions, diaries and account book, June-Nov. 1846, vol. 1, CHL, in *Mormon Midwife*, ed. Donna Toland Smart (Logan: Utah State University Press, 1997), 56–57, 59–67.
6. Mary Parker Richards to Samuel Whitney Richards, July 13, 1846, in *Winter Quarters*, ed. Maurine Carr Ward (Logan: Utah State University Press, 1996), 78.
7. Juanita Brooks, *A Mormon Chronicle* (San Marino, CA: Huntington Library Publications, 1955, 2003), 3.
8. John D. Lee, journal, Feb. 16, 1847, in Charles Kelly, ed., *Journals of John D. Lee, 1846–47 and 1859* (SLC: University of Utah Press, 1984), 80.
9. D&C 132:7; Woodruff, journal, July 24, 1846.
10. For examples, see Lee, journal, Feb. 16, 1847; Woodruff, journal, Aug. 2, 1846.
11. Book of Common Prayer, 149–51.
12. Juanita Brooks, *John Doyle Lee* (Glendale, CA: Arthur H. Clark, 1962), 378–82.
13. Lee, journal, Jan. 25; Mar. 10, 12, and 17, 1847.
14. Lee, journal, July 19, 1847; Smith, *Revelation, Resistance, and Mormon Polygamy*, 215–19.
15. Ulrich, *House Full of Females*, 151–52.
16. Benjamin F. Johnson, *My Life's Review* (Independence, MO: Zion's Printing and Publishing, 1947), 106.
17. Ulrich, *House Full of Females*, 193.

Chapter 4: Growth of Polygamy in the West (1847–81)

1. Howard Stansbury, *Exploration and Survey of the Valley of the Great Salt Lake of Utah* (Philadelphia: Lippincott, Grambo, & Co., 1852), 137.
2. Orson Pratt, "Celestial Marriage," Aug. 29, 1852, *JD*, 1:53–54;

David J. Whittaker, "The Bone in the Throat," *Western Historical Quarterly* 18, no. 3 (July 1987): 301.

3. Pratt, "Celestial Marriage," *JD*, 1:54.
4. Richard Ballantyne to Huldah Meriah Ballantyne, Sept. 6, 1853, 1, CHL. See also R. Lanier Britsch, "The East India Mission of 1851–56," *Journal of Mormon History* 27, no. 2 (Fall 2001): 167–69.
5. Fanny Stenhouse, *Exposé of Polygamy in Utah* (New York: American News, 1872), 34.
6. In the nineteenth century, the term *celestial marriage* was synonymous with *plural marriage*. The context of this quote makes clear that Spencer is referring to plural marriage. Emily B. Spencer, "Polygamy," *WE* 7, no. 14 (Dec. 15, 1878): 107.
7. George married Mary Ann Payne in 1855 (seven children) and Sarah Marinda Thompson in 1858 (six children). George Spencer (ID: KVPR-Z51) and Emily Brown Bush (ID: KWJ2-3X1), www.familysearch.org.
8. Brigham Young, "Provo Conference," *Deseret News*, Nov. 14, 1855, 282.
9. See Paul H. Peterson, "The Mormon Reformation of 1856–1857," *Journal of Mormon History* 15 (1989): 59–87; Thomas G. Alexander, "Wilford Woodruff and the Mormon Reformation of 1855–57," *Dialogue* 15 no. 3 (Summer 1992), 25–39.
10. Hannah Tapfield King, "Autobiography," 142–43, CHL.
11. Joseph Cluff to Brigham Young, Feb. 14, 1861, CHL.
12. Heber C. Kimball to James Snow, Mar. 6, 1857, CHL.
13. Emma R. Conover, "Autobiographical Sketch," 1908, 4, CHL; emphasis in original.
14. Kathryn M. Daynes, *More Wives Than One* (Urbana and Chicago: University of Illinois Press, 2001), 100–101, 165–66.
15. Sarah Sturtevant Leavitt, "Autobiography," 1875, in *History of Sarah Studevant Leavitt*, ed. Juanita L. Pulsipher (n.p., 1919), http://www.boap.org/LDS/Early-Saints/SLeavitt.html.

Chapter 5: The Antipolygamy Crusade (1882–90)

1. Zina D. H. Young, "One Who Knows," *WE* 11, no. 21 (Apr. 1, 1883): 161.
2. *Proceedings of the First Three Republican National Conventions* (Minneapolis: Charles W. Johnson, 1893), 43.
3. "The Manifesto and the End of Plural Marriage," Gospel Topics Essays, www. churchofjesuschrist.org; *Reynolds v. United States*, 98 U.S. 145 (1879).
4. Edwin Brown Firmage and Richard Collin Mangrum, *Zion in the Courts* (Urbana: University of Illinois Press, 1988, repr. 2001), 139; Gary Vitale, "Abraham Lincoln and the Mormons," *Journal of the Illinois State Historical Society* 101, nos. 3/4 (2008): 260–71.
5. A Bill in Aid of the Execution of the Laws in the Territory of Utah,

and for Other Purposes, H.R. 696, 41st Cong., 2nd Sess. [1870]; Van Wagoner, *Mormon Polygamy*, 108–10.

6. See Sarah Barringer Gordon, *The Mormon Question* (Chapel Hill: University of North Carolina Press, 2002).
7. Jill Mulvay Derr, Janath Russell Cannon, and Maureen Ursenbach Beecher, *Women of Covenant* (SLC: Deseret Book; Provo, UT: Brigham Young University Press, 1992), 75–80, 86–94.
8. "Great Indignation Meeting," *Deseret Evening News*, Jan. 14, 1870.
9. "The Mormon Women in Council," *New York Herald*, Jan. 23, 1870.
10. See Carol Cornwall Madsen, ed., *Battle for the Ballot* (Logan: Utah State University Press, 1997); Lola Van Wagenen, *Sister-Wives and Suffragists* (Provo, UT: BYU Studies, 2003).
11. Zina Young Williams, diary, Jan. 26, 1879, CHL.
12. John Taylor, "Comprehensiveness of the Lord's Prayer," Jan. 4, 1880, *JD*, 21:70–71.
13. Kenneth D. Driggs, "The Prosecutions Begin," *Dialogue* 21, no. 1 (Spring 1988): 112.
14. Herbert Elliot Woolley quoted in Kimberly Jensen James, "Between Two Fires," *Journal of Mormon History* 8 (1981): 49. Original in Herbert Elliot Woolley, "My Reflections," 4, BYU.
15. "Declaration and Protest to the President and People of the United States," in *"Mormon" Protest against Injustice* (SLC: Jos. Hyrum Parry, 1885), 22.
16. Annie Gardner, interview by James Hulett, n.d., 3, BYU.
17. Melvin L. Bashore estimated there were more than 1,300 incarcerated Mormon polygamists in prisons in Arizona, Michigan, South Dakota, Idaho, and Utah ("Life Behind Bars," *Utah Historical Quarterly* 47, no. 1 [Winter 1979]: 24). Rosa Mae M. Evans projected that 940 men were imprisoned on charges relating to polygamy in Utah ("Judicial Prosecution of Prisoners for LDS Plural Marriage" [master's thesis, Brigham Young University, 1986], 3).
18. George Kirkham (ID: KWZK-HFT), journals, Dec. 8, 1886; Mar. 12 and 21, 1887, 454, 462–64, www.familysearch.org.
19. Daynes, *More Wives Than One*, 98–100.
20. Annie Clark Tanner, *A Mormon Mother*, 4th ed. (SLC: University of Utah Tanner Trust Fund, 2006), 66.
21. Mary Elizabeth Woolley Chamberlain, "A Sketch of My Life," in *Mary E. Woolley Chamberlain*, comp. Farel Chamberlain Kimball (Provo, UT: privately published, 1981), 176, 181–82.
22. Daynes, *More Wives Than One*, 100–101; Stanley S. Ivins, "Notes on Mormon Polygamy," *Utah Historical Quarterly* 35, no. 4 (1967): 311–13.
23. "Remarks Made by President Wilford Woodruff," *Deseret Evening News*, Nov. 7, 1891. There has been disagreement, then and now, over whether Wilford Woodruff's 1890 Manifesto was a revelation or an administrative action of the Church. It is now interpreted to be a revelation. "The Manifesto and the End of Plural Marriage,"

Gospel Topics Essays; B. Carmon Hardy, *Solemn Covenant* (Urbana: University of Illinois Press, 1992), 146–52.

24. *Late Corporation of the Church of Jesus Christ of Latter-Day Saints v. United States*, 136 U.S. 1 (1890).
25. Woodruff, journal, Sept. 25, 1890.
26. Andrew J. Hansen, "Autobiography," [1911–32], 48, CHL.
27. "General Conference: Third Day," *Deseret Evening News*, Oct. 6, 1890; Joseph H. Dean, journal, Oct. 6, 1890, 118–20, CHL.
28. Dean, journal, 120; John Whittaker, diaries, Oct. 6, 1890, 10, Marriott Library Special Collections, University of Utah, SLC.
29. Gardner, interview by Hulett, 4. Bishop Orson F. Whitney read the Manifesto in general conference, not Wilford Woodruff. "General Conference: Third Day."
30. Tanner, *Mormon Mother*, 130.
31. Lorena Eugenia Washburn Larsen, "Life Sketch of Lorena Eugenia Washburn Larsen," ca. 1939, 239–41, BYU.

Chapter 6: Post-Manifesto and Beyond

1. Emmeline B. Wells, diary, Oct. 9, 1890, vol. 13, BYU.
2. John B. Fairbanks to Lillie Fairbanks, Oct. 12, 1890, CHL.
3. Lillie Fairbanks to John B. Fairbanks, Oct. 21, 1890, CHL.
4. John B. Fairbanks to Lillie Fairbanks, Nov. 9, 1890, CHL.
5. "The Manifesto and the End of Plural Marriage," Gospel Topics Essays.
6. Kenneth L. Cannon II, "Beyond the Manifesto," *Utah Historical Quarterly* 46, no. 1 (Winter 1978): 24–36.
7. US House of Representatives, "Admission of Utah," 52nd Congress, 2nd Session. Reports of Committees, 24 Jan. 1893. (Washington: Government Printing Office 1893), 3.
8. See A. J. Hansen, "Autobiography," 51.
9. See Jean B. White, *Charter for Statehood*, Utah Centennial Series, vol. 9 (SLC: University of Utah Press, 1996).
10. Utah State Constitution, article 3.
11. See Kathleen Flake, *Politics of American Religious Identity* (Chapel Hill: University of North Carolina Press, 2004).
12. Conference Report, Apr. 1904, 75.
13. Of the nineteen members of the Quorum of the Twelve who served between 1890 and 1904, eight married new plural wives between those years. See "The Manifesto and the End of Plural Marriage," Gospel Topics Essays; Flake, *Politics of American Religious Identity*, 92–108.
14. Hardy, *Solemn Covenant*, 327–28.
15. Gordon B. Hinckley, "What Are People Asking about Us?" *Ensign*, Nov. 1998.

Chapter 7: How Did Polygamy Work?

1. Amasa Lyman, "Marriage: Its Benefits," Apr. 5, 1866, *JD*, 11:207.

2. Woodruff, journal, July 24, 1846; Daynes, *More Wives Than One*, 192.
3. John Taylor, "Hostility of the World to the Gospel," Feb. 12, 1882, *JD*, 26:95; John Taylor, "Truth Always the Same," June 24, 1883, *JD*, 24:269.
4. Orson Pratt, "Celestial Marriage," *The Seer* 1, no. 2 (Feb. 1853): 31.
5. Taylor, "Truth Always the Same," 269–70.
6. Joseph Harker to Brigham Young, Feb. 1, 1857, CHL.
7. Brigham Young to Peter Shirts, Feb. 13, 1860, CHL.
8. Pratt, "Celestial Marriage," *Seer*, 1:31.
9. Vicky Burgess-Olson, "Family Structures and Dynamics in Early Utah Mormon Families, 1847–1885" (PhD diss., Northwestern University, 1975), 108.
10. See Pratt, "Celestial Marriage," *Seer*, 1:31, 41; Daynes, *More Wives Than One*, 65.
11. Ruth May Fox, interview by James Hulett, Mar. 16, 1935, 4, BYU.
12. Mary E. Croshaw Farrell, interview by James Hulett, Mar. 3, 1937, 2, BYU.
13. Rachel Emma Woolley Simmons, journal, vol. 1, 68–70, CHL.
14. Pratt, "Celestial Marriage," *Seer*, 1:31–32.
15. If the first wife did not give permission or personal circumstances did not allow her presence, the ceremony would proceed without her. This was particularly true during the Raid, when ceremonies were conducted with greater secrecy to avoid implicating first wives.
16. Pratt, "Celestial Marriage," *Seer*, 1:31–32.
17. The 1890 US Census burned; thus statistics for that year are not available. Daynes, *More Wives Than One*, 101.
18. Utah's population was 40,273 in 1860; 86,786 in 1870; 143,963 in 1880; and 207,905 in 1890; and 276,749 in 1900. "Population of Utah by Counties and Minor Civil Divisions," *Census Bulletin* 50 (Feb. 4, 1901): 1.
19. United Order communities lived the law of consecration and members had all things in common. L. Dwight Israelsen, "United Orders," in *Encyclopedia of Mormonism* (New York: Macmillan, 1992), 1494–95.
20. Lowell "Ben" Bennion, "The Incidence of Mormon Polygamy in 1880," *Journal of Mormon History* 11 (1984): 31.
21. Marie Cornwall, Camela Courtright, and Laga Van Beck, "How Common the Principle? Women as Plural Wives in 1860," *Dialogue* 26, no. 2 (Summer 1993): 139–53. See also Lowell C. "Ben" Bennion, "Mapping the Extent of Plural Marriage in St. George, 1861–1880," *BYU Studies Quarterly* 51, no. 4 (2012): 46–47.
22. Leonard Arrington and Davis Bitton, *The Mormon Experience*, 2nd ed. (Chicago: University of Illinois Press, 1992), 204.
23. Ivins, "Notes on Mormon Polygamy," 313–14.
24. Jessie L. Embry, *Mormon Polygamous Families* (SLC: University of Utah Press, 1987), 34–35.
25. Ivins, "Notes on Mormon Polygamy," 315.

26. Embry, *Mormon Polygamous Families*, 34–35.
27. Martha S. Heywood, journals, Jan. 16, 1852, vol. 1, CHL.
28. Daynes, *More Wives Than One*, 63.
29. Mary Jane McCleve Meeks, interview, in Harold H. Jenson, "True Pioneer Stories," *The Instructor*, Mar. 1932, 137.
30. Priddy Meeks, journal, 44–45, BYU.
31. Kirstine Christensen Baird to unknown recipient, n.d., private possession.
32. C. R. Savage, letter to the editor, "Anything for Money," *Deseret News*, Jan. 7, 1880.
33. W. Randall Dixon, "The Beehive and Lion Houses," in *Brigham Young's Homes*, ed. Colleen Whitley (Logan: Utah State University Press, 2002), chap. 6.
34. In Annie Laurie, "First Senator among Women," *San Francisco Examiner,* Nov. 9, 1896.
35. Walter M. Gallichan, *Women under Polygamy* (London: Holden and Hardingham, 1914), 308.
36. Daynes, *More Wives Than One*, 128.
37. Daynes, *More Wives Than One*, 130–33.
38. Clarissa Harden Wilhelm, diary, 1888–1895, 19, BYU.
39. Elizabeth Kane, *A Gentile Account of Life in Utah's Dixie, 1872–73*, ed. Norman R. Bowen and Mary Karen Bowen Solomon (SLC: Tanner Trust Fund, University of Utah Library, 1995), 39.
40. See "The Women of Utah: No. 3," *Anti-Polygamy Standard*, June 1880, 18.
41. Laurie, "First Senator among Women."
42. Christine T. Cox, "The Hand of the Diligent Maketh Rich," in *Women of Faith in the Latter Days, Volume 3 (1846–1870)*, ed. Richard E. Turley Jr. and Brittany A. Chapman (SLC: Deseret Book, 2014), 202.
43. Smith, *Revelation, Resistance, and Polygamy*, 238–39.
44. Josephine Streeper Chase, diary, June 19, 1881, Marriott Library Special Collections.
45. Daynes, *More Wives Than One*, 141.
46. Jane Snyder Richards, Reminiscences of Mrs. F. D. Richards, 1880, 64, Bancroft Library, University of California, Berkeley.
47. Daynes, *More Wives Than One*, 154.
48. President's Office Journal, Oct. 5, 1861, qtd. in Van Wagoner, *Mormon Polygamy*, 93.
49. Daynes, *More Wives Than One*, 159.
50. Jeffrey Ogden Johnson, "Determining and Defining 'Wife,'" *Dialogue* 20, no. 3 (Fall 1987): 57–70; Lisa Olsen Tait, "A Modern Patriarchal Family," in *Joseph F. Smith: Reflections on the Man and His Times*, ed. Craig K. Manscill, Brian D. Reeves, Guy L. Dorius, and J. B. Haws (Provo, UT: Religious Studies Center; SLC: Deseret Book, 2013), 74–95.
51. Daynes, *More Wives Than One,* 143.

52. Hannah Thompson Winder Brower, autobiography, ca. 1911, 30, CHL.
53. Daynes, *More Wives Than One*, 160.
54. Eugene E. Campbell and Bruce L. Campbell, "Divorce among Mormon Polygamists," *Utah Historical Quarterly* 46:1 (Winter 1978): 5.
55. Daynes, *More Wives Than One*, 161.
56. Daynes, *More Wives Than One*, 163.
57. Tanner, *Mormon Mother*, 236.
58. Mary Mount Tanner to Matilda Coley Griffing Bancroft, Oct. 24, 1880, Bancroft Library.

Chapter 8: Why Practice Polygamy?

1. "Grapes from Thorns, and Figs from Thistles," *Millennial Star* 1, no. 9 (Jan. 1841): 238; Grant Underwood, *The Millenarian World of Early Mormonism* (Urbana and Chicago: University of Illinois Press, 1999).
2. Sarah Barnes Layton, "Autobiography of Sarah B. Layton," *WE* 29, nos. 12–13 (Nov. 15 and Dec. 1, 1900): 55–56.
3. Ruth May Fox, "My Story," 1953, 20, CHL.
4. Alma Don Sorensen and Valerie Hudson Cassler, *Women in Eternity, Women of Zion* (Springville, UT: Cedar Fort, 2004), 189–206.
5. John Taylor, "Scope of the Gospel," June 18, 1883, *JD*, 24:197. See also Larry E. Dahl, "The Abrahamic Test," in *Sperry Symposium Classics: The Old Testament*, ed. Paul Y. Hoskisson (Provo, UT: Religious Studies Center; SLC: Deseret Book, 2005), 83–99.
6. Artimesia Snow, "Address," *WE* 11, no. 10 (Oct. 15, 1882): 77.
7. See Matt. 16:19; Hel. 10:7; D&C 128:9; 132:7, 13–14; Bushman, *Rough Stone Rolling*, 497.
8. Smith, "Plural Marriage," 26–31; Daynes, *More Wives Than One*, 71–76, 73n31.
9. Brigham Young, "Delegate Hooper," Aug. 19, 1866, *JD*, 11:268–69; italics added.
10. Wilford Woodruff, diary, Sept. 24, 1871, CHL.
11. John Hawley, autobiography, 43, Community of Christ Archives, Independence, MO.
12. John Hawley later converted to the Reorganized Church of Jesus Christ of Latter Day Saints. This denomination did not practice plural marriage. Melvin C. Johnson, *Life and Times of John Pierce Hawley* (Draper, UT: Greg Kofford, 2019).
13. See Benjamin F. Johnson to George F. Gibbs, Apr. 1903–Oct. 1911, 35, CHL; Heber C. Kimball to Vilate Kimball, Feb. 12, 1849, CHL; Hales, *Joseph Smith's Polygamy*, 3:165–69, 245–52.
14. Wilford Woodruff to Samuel Amos Woolley, May 22, 1888, qtd. in Hales, *Joseph Smith's Polygamy*, 3:218.
15. Marcus B. Nash, "The New and Everlasting Covenant," *Ensign*, Dec. 2015. See also Pratt, "Celestial Marriage," *Seer*, 1:32.
16. Brigham Young was actually sealed to fifty-five women during his lifetime, and most of these relationships were not conjugal. Twenty-three

wives became members of his household, and he fathered fifty-six children by sixteen different wives. Johnson, "Determining and Defining 'Wife,'" 57–60.

17. Priscilla Merriman Evans, "Records of the Handcart Pioneers," *Our Pioneer Heritage*, comp. Kate B. Carter (SLC: Daughters of Utah Pioneers, 1971), 14:282.
18. Whitney, *Why We Practice Plural Marriage*, 56–57; Ulrich, *House Full of Females*, 100; "Incidents in the Life of Mrs. Harrington," *Deseret Evening News*, June 26, 1912.
19. "Plural Marriage in The Church of Jesus Christ of Latter-day Saints," Gospel Topics Essays.
20. Clarissa Harden Wilhelm, diary, 1888–1895, 19, BYU.
21. "Margaret McNeil Ballard," Happenings in the Valley, in *Our Pioneer Heritage* (SLC: Daughters of Utah Pioneers, 1960), 3:203.
22. Joan Iversen, "Feminist Implications of Mormon Polygyny," *Feminist Studies* 10, no. 3 (Autumn 1984): 508.
23. Elizabeth Graham Macdonald, autobiography, 1875, 44, CHL.
24. See Brigham Young, "Secret of Happiness," June 23, 1874, *JD*, 18:249; Orson Spencer, *Patriarchal Order, or Plurality of Wives!* (Liverpool: S. W. Richards, 1853), 16.
25. Hales, *Joseph Smith's Polygamy*, 3:151–60.
26. Kane, *Gentile Account*, 20–21.
27. Daynes, *More Wives Than One*, 110–13.
28. Augusta Joyce Crocheron, "Louie B. Felt," in *Representative Women of Deseret* (SLC: J. C. Graham, 1884), 58.
29. Alma Elizabeth Mineer Felt, interview by James Hulett, May 9, 1937, 1, BYU.
30. Kirkham, journals, May 1, 1875.
31. Ida Francis Hunt Udall, journal, 27–28, Merrill-Cazier Library, Utah State University, Logan.
32. Taylor, "Hostility of the World," 26:95.

Chapter 9: Personal Journeys of Faith

1. John Taylor, "President John Taylor's Recent Trip to Bear Lake," 1883, *JD*, 24:230–31.
2. Jeanette Irvine McMurrin, "Autobiographical Sketch," n.d., 3, CHL; Cherry B. Silver, "I Obeyed the Call," chap. 36, in *Women of Faith in the Latter Days, Volume 2*, ebook.
3. Cordelia Morley Cox, "Collection of Biographies, ca. 1880," BYU.
4. Else Marie [Mary] Christensen Hansen (ID: KWNV-K99), autobiography, 2, www.familysearch.org.
5. A. J. Hansen, "Autobiography," 40.
6. E. M. Hansen, autobiography, 2.
7. A. J. Hansen, "Autobiography," 41.
8. "Autobiography of Sarah B. Layton," *WE* 29, nos. 22–23 (Apr. 15 and May 1, 1901): 97.
9. Marian Cannon Nelson Warner, "In Search of the Mousley Heritage,

1884–1900," in *In Search of the Mousley Heritage*, comp. Angus M. Cannon Reunion Committee, 29, CHL.
10. Silas Derryfield Smith, "Life Story," in *Silas Derryfield Smith, 1867 to 1956*, comp. Derryfield N. Smith, Ethel Smith Randall, and Seraphine Smith Frost (Mesa, AZ: privately printed, 1970), 34, CHL.
11. Macdonald, autobiography, 43.
12. See Daynes, *More Wives Than One*, 61–65.
13. Leavitt, "Autobiography."
14. Hawley, autobiography, 59–60.

Chapter 10: Relationship between Husband and Wives

1. More Anon, "A Mormon Woman's Views," *WE* 13 (Nov. 1, 1884): 81.
2. Phineas W. Cook, reminiscences and journal, vol. 1, 74, CHL.
3. Macdonald, autobiography, 40.
4. Brigham Young, "The United Order Is the Order of the Kingdom," Aug. 9, 1874, *JD*, 17:160.
5. David Candland, autobiography and diary, ca. 1841–1900, Mar. 1859, 63, Mormonism and the West, Huntington Digital Library, http://hdl.huntington.org.
6. Richard Ballantyne, journal, Mar. 27, 1886, vol. 7, CHL.
7. John J. Esplin, interview by James Hulett, ca. Feb. 1935, 4, BYU.
8. Mary Jane Mount Tanner to Mary Bessac Hunt, Oct. 7, 1883, in *A Fragment: The Autobiography of Mary Jane Mount Tanner*, ed. Margery W. Ward (SLC: Tanner Trust Fund, University of Utah Library, 1980), 200.
9. Oluf Larsen, "A Biographical Sketch of the Life of Oluf Christian Larsen," 52, CHL.
10. Tanner, *Mormon Mother*, 270–71.
11. Felt, interview by Hulett, Mar. 26, 1935, 6.
12. More Anon, "Mormon Woman's Views," 82.
13. Mrs. Joseph Horne, "Migration and Settlement of the Latter Day Saints," 1884, 34–35, Bancroft Library.
14. See Suzanne Adel Katz, "Sisters in Salvation" (master's thesis, California State University, Fullerton, 1987), www.familysearch.org.
15. Emily E. Hart, diaries, Jan. 30, 1862, CHL.
16. Jane R. Hindley, journals, Dec. 11, 1862, CHL.
17. Hindley, journals, Dec. 22, 1862.
18. Caroline Chappell Nelson to William W. Nelson, Feb. 29, 1880, 1–2, CHL.
19. George William Tripp, "Biographical Sketch of Caroline C. W. N. Brown," n.d., 5, CHL.
20. Emma Wartstill Mecham Nielson, diary, Aug. 26, 1887, 14, BYU.
21. Candland, autobiography and diary, Feb. 1859, 61.
22. Emmeline B. Wells, diary, vol. 14, Mar. 26, 1891, 115, BYU.
23. Wells, diary, vol. 2, Sept. 30, 1874, 50–51.
24. Martha Hughes Cannon to Barbara Replogle, Aug. 10, 1888, CHL.
25. Kane, *Gentile Account*, 123.

26. Sarah A. Cooke, interview by Matilda C. Bancroft, 1884, "Theatrical and Social Affairs in Utah: SLC," 5–6; original at Bancroft Library.
27. Kane, *Gentile Account*, 123.
28. Esther Anderson Huntsman, interview by James Hulett, Apr. 9, 1937, 12, BYU.
29. Parley P. Pratt to Ann Agatha Pratt, June 24, 1852, CHL.
30. Ann Agatha Pratt to Parley P. Pratt, July 18, 1854, CHL.
31. "Reminiscences of Mrs. A. Agatha Pratt," 1907, 1, CHL; see also Ann Agatha Pratt to Parley P. Pratt, 1847–1857, CHL; [Belinda Marden Pratt], *Defence of Polygamy* (n.p., 1854), 8.
32. Smith, "Life Story," 38.
33. Laura Moffet Jones, interview by James Hulett, Oct. 22, 1935, 4–5, BYU.
34. Wells, diary, Mar. 13, 1890, vol. 13, 96.
35. Wells, diary, Mar. 26, 1891, vol. 14, 115.
36. E. M. Hansen, autobiography, 2–3.

Chapter 11: Relationships among Wives

1. Ida Hunt to Eliza Luella Udall, Jan. 29, 1882, CHL.
2. Eliza Luella Udall to Ida Francis Hunt, Mar. 12, 1882, CHL.
3. Spencer, "Polygamy," 107.
4. Adelia A. Wilcox Kimball, reminiscences, n.d., 39–42, 46, CHL.
5. Larsen, "Life Sketch," 144–45.
6. Sarah Ann Obray Smith [Mrs. Orson Smith], interview by James Hulett, Mar. 25, 1937, 21, BYU.
7. Martha Cragun Cox, autobiography, 1928–1930, 126, CHL.
8. Chamberlain, "Sketch of My Life," 175.
9. Helen Marr Clark Callister, speech, ca. 1878, 2, CHL.
10. Elizabeth Kane, *Twelve Mormon Homes Visited in Succession on a Journey through Utah to Arizona* (Philadelphia: n.p., 1874), 52–53.
11. Kane, *Twelve Mormon Homes*, 52.
12. Macdonald, autobiography, 41.
13. Ellis R. Shipp, "Third Book of Life Sketches: All in the Rough," 50, Utah State Historical Society, SLC.
14. Susan Evans McCloud, "'Those Who Love Most Tenderly Are Surely Most Like Thee': Ellis Reynolds Shipp (1847–1939)," in *Women of Faith in the Latter Days, Volume 3*, 179–82.
15. Peter Nielsen (ID: KWJ8-GWM), May 5, 1867, journal, in "Translation of History of Peter Nielsen Written by Myself," 236, www.familysearch.org.
16. Kate B. Carter, comp., "The Other Mother," Daughters of Utah Pioneers Lesson for December 1937, 12.
17. Cox, autobiography, 133.
18. Agatha Walker McAllister (ID: KW8Z-4F4), "Memoirs," 11, www.familysearch.org.
19. "Autobiography of Sarah B. Layton," *WE* 30 (Sept. 1901): 30.
20. Fox, interview by Hulett, 4.

21. Macdonald, autobiography, 40.
22. Esther Romania Bunnell Pratt Penrose, memoir, 1881, 6, CHL.

Chapter 12: Family Relationships

1. Artimesia Beaman Snow to Erastus Snow, Apr. 30, 1855, in "Erastus Snow Family Personal Letters," ed. Don Snow, Utah Valley Technology and Genealogy Group, http://uvtagg.org.
2. Cox, autobiography, 131–32.
3. Edna Lambson Smith to Joseph F. Smith, Apr. 6, 1874, CHL.
4. Julina Smith, "A Loving Tribute to Sarah Ellen Richards Smith," *Relief Society Magazine*, May 1915, 215.
5. Joseph W. Pratt, interview by Marsha C. Martin, Oct. 22, 1982, 3–4, BYU.
6. Annie Richardson Johnson, interview by Leonard R. Grover, Apr. 23, 1980, 6, BYU.
7. Macdonald, autobiography, 40.
8. Emeline Grover Rich, diary, Dec. 31, 1893, CHL.
9. Nielson, diary, Aug. 26, 1887, 13–14.
10. Nielson, diary, Jan. 3, 1891, 55.
11. Cooke, interview by Bancroft, 5–6.
12. Ellen Pratt McGary to Ellen Spencer Clawson, Aug. 6, 1857, in *Dear Ellen*, ed. S. George Ellsworth (SLC: Tanner Trust Fund, University of Utah Library, 1974), 43.
13. Olive Andelin Potter, "Autobiography," 8, BYU.
14. Archie L. Jenkins, interview by Leonard Grover, Feb. 16, 1980, 15, BYU.
15. Hiram B. Clawson to "My Dear Wives," May 24, 1858, Marriott Library Special Collections.
16. H. W. Naisbitt, "Marriage Ordained of God," Mar. 8, 1885, *JD*, 26:124.
17. Juanita Brooks, "A Close-Up of Polygamy," *Harper's Monthly*, Feb. 1934, 306.
18. M. E. Talmage, "An Indignant Mormon Mother," *WE* 12, no. 14 (Dec. 15, 1883): 109.
19. Felt, interview by Hulett, May 9, 1937, 3.

Conclusion: What Does Polygamy Mean for Latter-day Saints Today?

1. "Plural Marriage and Families in Early Utah," Gospel Topics Essays.
2. Family History Department, "Analysis of Historical Plural Marriages in The Church of Jesus Christ of Latter-day Saints according to Family Tree," 2018, unpublished research, quoted by Matthew J. Grow, in "Worldwide Devotional for Young Adults: A Face to Face Event with Elder Quentin L. Cook" (broadcast, Nauvoo, IL, Sept. 9, 2018), www.churchofjesuschrist.org.
3. Felt, interview by Hulett, Mar. 26, 1935, 6.
4. "Polygamy," Newsroom, https://newsroom.churchofjesuschrist.org.

5. Ezra Taft Benson, "Fourteen Fundamentals in Following the Prophet," *Liahona*, June 1981.
6. Quentin L. Cook, "Church History: A Source of Strength and Inspiration," *Ensign*, July 2020, 16.
7. Marcus B. Nash, "The New and Everlasting Covenant," *Ensign*, December 2015.
8. Dallin H. Oaks, "Trust in the Lord," *Ensign*, Nov. 2019.
9. "Plural Marriage in Kirtland and Nauvoo," Gospel Topics Essays.
10. "Sealing Policies," General Handbook, July 2020, 38.5.1.3, 38.5.1.7, www.churchofjesuschrist.org.
11. Relief Society minute book, Lehi Ward, Alpine Stake, Oct. 27, 1869, CHL.
12. Joseph B. Wirthlin, "Come What May, and Love It," *Ensign*, Nov. 2008.
13. Carole M. Stephens, "The Family is of God," *Ensign*, May 2015.
14. Sarah Comstock, "The Mormon Woman," *Collier's: The National Weekly* 44 (Nov. 6, 1909): 17.
15. See Edward L. Kimball, "The History of LDS Temple Admission Standards," *Journal of Mormon History* 24, no. 1 (Spring 1998): 139, 144–46.
16. "Church Policies and Guidelines," General Handbook, 38.4.4.
17. Russell M. Nelson, "Concluding Remarks," *Ensign*, Nov. 2019.

INDEX